PRAISE for
10 Steps to Take Charge of Your Emotional Life

"Learning to control emotions is both difficult and rewarding, probably one of the most important steps to attain optimum health of both mind and body. Dr. Eve Wood has authored a detailed and practical guide to help you do it. I recommend this book and am completely in agreement with the philosophy behind it."

— **Andrew Weil, M.D.,** director, University of Arizona Program in Integrative Medicine; clinical professor of medicine and public health; the author of *8 Weeks to Optimum Health* and *Healthy Aging*

"Psychiatrist Eve Wood, America's number one practitioner/educator in mental illness and integrative medicine, understands that our minds can't, don't, or won't always register the emotions that impact us so profoundly. Her long-awaited, authoritative new book is an outstanding resource for navigating the myriad mainstream and alternative options to empower the reader to make informed decisions about treatment choices. Dr. Wood has created a balanced work that health-care providers, patients with psychiatric diagnoses, and anyone interested in developing their mental wellness will find extremely useful."

— **Candace B. Pert, Ph.D.,** scientific director, RAPID Pharmaceuticals; and the author of *Molecules of Emotion* and *Everything You Need to Know to Feel Go(o)d*

"A clear, intelligent, and sensible guide to cultivating emotional health, integrating the best of holistic therapies with sound allopathic medical principles. Dr. Wood demystifies psychiatry without talking down to her readers, taking it that extra, badly needed step: She explains the cutting-edge mind-body therapies that are making such impressive inroads with what have traditionally been daunting mental-health challenges. A wonderful resource for those who want to know how to make smart, individualized choices that respect their unique needs and collaborate with their inborn abilities."

— **Belleruth Naparstek, LISW, BCD,** the author of *Invisible Heroes: Survivors of Trauma and How They Heal*

"This well-thought-out program will help you understand the origins and causes of your problems and show you how to address them. In ten steps, Eve Wood offers a wealth of suggestions, resources, and exercises for self-healing and consultation. I highly recommend this book to take charge of your emotional life."

— **Daniel J. Benor, M.D., ABHM,** the author of *Spiritual Healing: Scientific Validation of a Healing Revolution* and *How Can I Heal What Hurts?*

"10 Steps to Take Charge of Your Emotional Life by Eve Wood is the perfect bridge between what is . . . and what is possible. She inspires and empowers her readers to take on the essential role of manager in the healing process and gently guides them to live their best life."

— **Michelle May, M.D.,** the author of *Am I Hungry?*

"The book has the gentle spirit of a personal conversation about healing and wholeness with Dr. Wood. She shares practical wisdom and exercises derived from her professional and personal experience as a fellow traveler. 10 Steps to Take Charge of Your Emotional Life is a gift and a great resource."

— **Frederic C. Craigie, Ph.D.,** associate professor of community and family medicine, Dartmouth Medical School

"Dr. Eve Wood shines a gentle light on the complex world of emotional health and reveals a path to healing She offers a broad range of options and shows you how to use them wisely. I recommend this excellent resource for dealing with life's challenges, big and small."

— **Victoria Maizes, M.D.,** executive director, University of Arizona program in integrative medicine; associate professor of medicine, family medicine, and public health

"10 Steps to Take Charge of Your Emotional Life is a gift to our society! Eve Wood helps each of us find the personal answers we need to achieve a healthy life filled with happiness. I love this brilliant, insightful recipe for wellness!"

— **Susan H. Cooper, M.A., M.S.,** community group coordinator, Institute of Noetic Sciences, Tucson, AZ

AUTHOR'S NOTE

Many of the stories in this book are true accounts in which the names and identifying details have been changed to protect confidentiality. Others are composites drawn from years of clinical work. The latter are true to the spirit of the teaching, although not to the experience of any particular person.

10 STEPS

TO TAKE CHARGE

of YOUR EMOTIONAL

LIFE

10 STEPS

TO TAKE CHARGE

of YOUR EMOTIONAL

LIFE

OVERCOMING ANXIETY, DISTRESS,
AND DEPRESSION THROUGH
WHOLE-PERSON HEALING

EVE A. WOOD, M.D.

An *In One*™ Series Book

HAY HOUSE, INC.
Carlsbad, California
London • Sydney • Johannesburg
Vancouver • Hong Kong • New Delhi

Published and distributed in the United States by: Hay House, Inc.: www.hayhouse.com • *Published and distributed in Australia by:* Hay House Australia Pty. Ltd.: www.hayhouse.com.au • *Published and distributed in the United Kingdom by:* Hay House UK, Ltd.: www.hayhouse.co.uk • *Published and distributed in the Republic of South Africa by:* Hay House SA (Pty), Ltd.: orders@psdprom.co.za • *Distributed in Canada by:* Raincoast: www.raincoast.com • *Published in India by:* Hay House Publications (India) Pvt. Ltd.: www.hayhouseindia.co.in

Editorial supervision: Jill Kramer • *Design:* Tricia Breidenthal • Index: Richard Comfort

In One™ is a trademark of Eve A. Wood, M.D. It symbolizes the imperative to treat body, mind, and spirit in one, as well as the affirmation that the Divine resides within each one of us. *In One*™ represents Dr. Wood's perspective and approach to healing.

Library of Congress Cataloging-in-Publication Data

Wood, Eve A.
  10 steps to take charge of your emotional life overcoming anxiety, distress, and depression through whole-person healing / Eve A. Wood.
    p. cm.
  Includes index.
  ISBN-13: 978-1-4019-1121-8 (hardcover)
  ISBN-13: 978-1-4019-1122-5 (tradepaper) 1. Alternative medicine. 2. Mind and body therapies. 3. Medicine and psychology. I. Title: Ten steps to take charge of your emotional life overcoming anxiety, distress, and depression through whole-person healing. II. Title.
  R733.W645 2007
  616--dc22   2006007984

Hardcover ISBN: 978-1-4019-1121-8
Tradepaper ISBN: 978-1-4019-1122-5

10 09 08 07   4 3 2 1
1st edition, January 2007

Printed in the United States of America

⸎

*In loving memory of my dearly departed father,
Leonard Wood, a gifted storyteller who: lived on the
sunny side of life, was always thrilled to hear from
me, routinely asked, "What can I do to help?" and
never failed to end a conversation with "I love you."*

*Dad, you know this book is for you. We spoke of its
dedication as you lay dying, ecstatic that I would have
the opportunity to help so many people! You had a
wondrous way of viewing life and its many challenges.*

*I carry your wisdom, humor, love, and support in my heart.
Your presence and memory are true blessings in my life.
Thank you for all that you've given me. May you rest in peace.*

Amen.

⸎

❧ CONTENTS

Introduction xiii

STEP 1:   Consider Your Story and Its Lessons: Do You Have
          a Medical Condition or a Chemical Imbalance? 1

STEP 2:   Explore Your Need for Medication. 31

STEP 3:   Follow Treatment Guidelines
          When Medication Is Necessary 49

STEP 4:   Include Complementary- and Alternative-
          Medicine Interventions 61

STEP 5:   Make Life Choices That Fit Your Nature 89

STEP 6:   Identify the Beliefs That Imprison You, and
          Reprogram the Brain Circuits Involved. 111

STEP 7:   Learn the Language of Your Body and
          Make Friends with Your Inner Healer 133

STEP 8:   Share Stories and Build Connections. 153

STEP 9:   Live in the Power of the Possible. 173

STEP 10: Nurture Your Spirit 193

Afterword 217
Glossary 221
Index 225
Acknowledgments 233
About the Author 235

INTRODUCTION

Congratulations on your decision to take charge of your emotional life! I'm glad to be partnering with you. No matter what your history or challenge, you can succeed. There's always hope.

Perhaps you've been trying to take charge for a long time but find yourself confused, lost, stuck, or not quite well. Or perhaps you've only recently become aware of your internal distress and aren't sure what to do about it. Maybe you've been diagnosed with a condition such as depression, attention deficit disorder (ADD), or panic disorder and wonder what you can do to best heal.

You may be taking medication but be unsure about whether you ought to do so, or you may not have a prescription and be wondering if you need one. You might be in therapy but question whether it's right for you, or without a therapist and feeling the need for one. You may realize that even when medication and/or therapy are necessary, they're only part of the healing puzzle. You may be taking herbs or supplements; engaging in yoga, meditation, or prayer; or watching what you eat and trying to support your wellness in other ways. You're probably confused about how to bring all these practices together in your life.

We live in very challenging times and are constantly bombarded with messages that raise one intervention up as the full answer. A TV commercial says: "Try medication and move from depressed to ecstatic." A practitioner's ad declares: "Enter therapy and transform your life." A yoga-studio brochure reads: "Begin a regular practice and you'll never need to do anything more." Our radios, televisions, and magazine pages overflow with advertisements for the ultimate medications, herbs, supplements, and mind-body or spiritual interventions. Each is touted as all you'll ever need for total well-being.

These messages often appeal to us because our health-care system is in a shambles. Most of us, even if we're lucky enough to have medical insurance, lack a long-term relationship with a doctor who knows us. A physician like the old TV character Dr. Marcus Welby—a friend, partner, and guide in life—is an ancient myth. We're wandering around dazed, with information overload. We have no idea where to turn for guidance; we don't even know who to trust.

My dear reader, I have good news for you: There's someone you can believe in, and there's a solution to this dilemma. There's a path through this maze, and you're ideally suited to find it. You can trust yourself—*you* are the answer! You can take charge of your emotional life, and I intend to teach you how.

You see, in the field of emotional and mental health, all diagnoses are made on the basis of your story and no one else's. We have no diagnostic tests in psychiatry. In other fields of medicine, a lung x-ray can find pneumonia, and blood analysis can find diabetes. But in the field of emotional well-being, only your report of symptoms—such as a depressed mood, sleep disturbance, hopelessness, and impaired concentration—can reveal depression.

Therefore, if you're given adequate information about the symptoms of common conditions, *you* can begin to figure out if you need medical assessment. Additionally, if you're given *enough* data about treatment and self-empowerment interventions, you can begin to find your own personal path to wellness, wholeness, and spiritual well-being. You can do so whether or not you have a known medical condition—you can find your way.

There's a right answer about what steps to take to promote healing and wellness, but it's *always* a *personal* solution. What makes sense for you may not be the best idea for your neighbor, spouse, sibling, or friend. Given enough information, guidance, and support, however, you'll find the keys to your own health. You can learn to tap into your inner healer and put together a "Take-Charge" program that fits your unique and wondrous being. You're the captain of your own ship, and I intend to teach you how to sail it.

10 Steps to Take Charge of Your Emotional Life is just what it sounds like. Each chapter walks you through one of the 10 steps. You'll find examples, stories, self-assessment questions, and guidance on what actions to take, based on your own unique situation and responses to the exercises. I've written a series of steps for you to visit and work on over time. Don't expect yourself to read each chapter once, implement all its lessons immediately, and totally transform your life by the time you finish reading the book. Taking charge is a process, and it takes a while. Here are the 10 steps involved:

Step 1: Consider your story and its lessons: Do you have a medical condition or chemical imbalance?

Step 2: Explore your need for medication.

Step 3: Follow treatment guidelines when medication is necessary.

Step 4: Include complementary and alternative interventions.

Step 5: Make life choices that fit your nature.

Step 6: Identify the beliefs that imprison you, and reprogram the brain circuits involved.

Step 7: Learn the language of your body, and make friends with your inner healer.

Step 8: Share stories and build connections.

Step 9: Live in the power of the possible.

Step 10: Nurture your spirit.

While I don't intend this book to be a substitute for medical care, psychotherapy, or other forms of treatment, I do mean for it to guide you through the Take-Charge process. I'll teach you how to bring your medical care, complementary and alternative approaches, self-help, and spiritual practices together for wellness.

You and only you can take charge of your emotional life—and you can succeed! In all my years of clinical practice, I've never met a single person who truly wanted to heal who couldn't. Where there's a will, there's always a way. In this book, I intend to show you how.

STEP 1

Consider Your Story and Its Lessons: Do You Have a Medical Condition or a Chemical Imbalance?

Welcome to Step 1 of your Take-Charge program. Perhaps you know the song "Do-Re-Mi" from *The Sound of Music*. In it, Maria teaches the importance of starting any project at the very beginning: When we learn to read, we begin with the ABCs; and when we sing, we begin with Do-Re-Mi. The first three actions just happen to be these initial stepping-stones. The only sensible place to start any journey is at its very beginning.

You've decided to take charge of your emotional life, but where should you begin? Which steps come first, and why? What are the ABCs or Do-Re-Mi of taking charge? Well, your initial plans are grounded in the field of medicine. They involve:

Step 1: Identifying the symptoms or problems that trouble you and figuring out which ones may be part of an illness or disorder

Step 2: Evaluating your need for medication intervention (whether you have a disorder or not)

Step 3: Learning how to use drugs properly, if they belong in your Take-Charge program

Oh boy, you may be thinking, *that doesn't sound like fun. And I don't want to have to take medicine. I don't like this idea one bit.* You may even be wondering why an integrative psychiatrist like me—who so values the role of love, energy, mind over matter, and spiritual pursuits—insists that you start your Take-Charge program with a medically based analysis of your symptoms and troubles. Why begin with the stuff that most of us view as a last resort?

Well, it turns out that many failed attempts at life transformation—most "stuckness," in fact—results from skipping over defining problems and implementing crucial interventions. You can read many stories that illustrate this problem in my first book, *There's Always Help; There's Always Hope.* All the mind-body tools in the world won't work if you're too depressed or anxious to use them. You'll set yourself up to fail if you try to do things that your mind isn't able to master because it's in a compromised state. So, you need to figure out if you have a diagnosis needing treatment.

You see, the process of taking charge of your emotional life is like building a house or planting a garden: You have to do a lot of things in a particular sequence in order to succeed. And although a lot of those early steps aren't particularly pretty or glitzy, you sure wouldn't want to miss them. For instance, in order to construct a sturdy home, you must dig and pour a foundation; in order to create a flowering oasis, you must fertilize and prepare your soil for seeds. When you build a house or create a garden, you have to do a lot of grunt work before you get to have fun—such as choosing carpet for your floors or cutting flowers for your table. Similarly, when taking charge of your emotional life, you'll need to do some exploring and groundwork before you can move into the steps that seem more appealing. You must start by examining your story for its lessons.

I've been a student and a doctor for many years, and I've been taught more facts than any one person could possibly remember. Occasionally, however, a teaching stands out. One such lesson is that the answer to the question *What's wrong with the patient, and what must be done to promote healing?* is contained in their original complaint and initial clinical history. When I listen carefully to my clients as they describe their challenges, and question them until I learn how they tick, I can often discover what's amiss—both diagnostically and holistically—and what they'll need to do to heal. The answers are in their stories.

In Step 1, you'll be considering your own story for diagnostic and treatment lessons. But you may not be sure what that means right now, so let's look at some examples of this process.

Expectations of Deterioration: Greg's Story

The first tale I want to tell you concerns an inappropriate diagnosis. Greg's label simply didn't fit his story. When this middle-aged veteran came to our integrative-medicine clinic as a patient, he was in a wheelchair. He was so weak that he was unable to lift a cup, for a debilitating illness had gripped him. He told us that he had Gulf War syndrome and post-traumatic stress disorder (PTSD). He'd read all about the former condition, and like the afflicted people he'd studied, he was becoming progressively weaker and more debilitated. He'd given up his job and almost everything else that gave him pleasure in life. He felt hopeless and only wanted to return to work. He wondered if we, in the integrative-medicine program, could help him.

As Greg told his story, his description of PTSD didn't sound accurate to me. I questioned him about his symptoms—and then it *definitely* didn't sound like he had that disorder, so I shared my thoughts with him: "I'm a psychiatrist, and as best as I can tell, it doesn't seem to me like you have PTSD. Maybe you aren't as ill as you think."

Several weeks later, Greg appeared for a follow-up visit. Only this time, he was walking and carrying his cup. He reported feeling better than he had for a long time, and he'd even taken on some work again. A medical student asked him what had happened to turn things around so much.

"Well," Greg said, "when that psychiatrist told me that I didn't have PTSD, I decided that maybe I shouldn't believe everything they were telling me at the VA. I decided to stop going there and to carry on as if I really were okay. It's made all the difference."

What's the lesson in this? Greg had become progressively more ill as he took on stories that didn't actually fit his own tale. He expected to worsen, so he did! But the diagnoses were incorrect. In choosing to throw out that faulty data, he was able to access his inner healer and find his own path to recovery. He was thus able to accomplish his goal of returning to work. The answers for combatting his problem were in his initial story: He didn't have what he thought he did.

The Origins of Pain: Jake's Story

Here's another example of "the answer is in the initial story"; this one concerns a missed diagnosis. Jake, also a middle-aged man, was referred to me for back pain and insomnia. On the phone, he told me that his pain was so severe that it would awaken him from sleep. He spent most days lying in bed, suffering and unable to do very much. Three years of extensive assessments and interventions had done little to improve his condition. His symptoms had been getting worse and worse over time, and when I spoke to him, he was feeling desperate.

I suggested that he read my first book, *There's Always Help; There's Always Hope,* before our initial visit two days hence. When he said: "I'd give anything for one good night's sleep," I told him that we'd start a long-acting sleep aid when he came in the following week.

When he arrived for his appointment, he told me that he'd read the book and, for the first time, realized that he had generalized anxiety disorder (GAD). He'd been a "worried guy" his whole life but never recognized that he had an anxiety-related illness. In taking his history, I discovered that he'd had a migrating series of physical symptoms over the years, such as headaches and stomach problems. This is common in GAD, and I felt that the body issues were part of his disorder.

Over the course of three visits, I was able to help Jake settle his agitated nervous system and calm his out-of-control anxiety disorder with medication. I also began to reframe his current pain. I told him to think about the sensation as psychological, not physical, since his back would hurt when he was upset about something. I urged him to wonder, *What is my body trying to tell me?* whenever the discomfort appeared. He was to stop focusing on his pain and searching for miracle remedies.

By Jake's fourth visit, he said, "I had a great week! I feel like myself again, and I was able to enjoy reading and being with my family. I haven't felt this well in months—maybe even years. I didn't have severe pain this week, so I could keep going. Thank you! I only wish I'd met you three years ago."

What's the lesson in this case? Again, the answer to the question *What's wrong?* is in the initial story. Although Jake was referred to me for insomnia and back pain, it quickly became clear to both of us—through knowing and learning his story—that his primary problem was an anxiety disorder that required appropriate treatment. The correct path became apparent once the proper identification had been made.

Lingering Grief: Rhonda's Story

A third example of "the answer is in the initial story" also concerns an unidentified diagnosis. During her first visit with me, a 37-year-old married woman named Rhonda said, "I don't understand what's wrong with me. Ever since the day my house was broken into, I've been unable to get my work done—I just can't concentrate. And what's worse, I don't even care! I'm not sleeping, food doesn't interest me, and I often think it would be easier if I could fall asleep forever when I go to bed. I'm not suicidal, but I don't see the point in going on; all I do is cry. None of this is usual for me. What do you think is wrong?"

Upon questioning Rhonda, I learned that her most cherished family photos and jewelry had been taken in the robbery. Her sense of safety and the connection to her past had been shattered, and grief had set in. Over time, the unprocessed emotion turned into a full-blown clinical depression. She was in my office because she was at the end of her rope. The condition was so big that nothing could interrupt it. She needed professional help to shift her brain chemistry enough to enable her to resume life and process her losses.

Her initial story dictated her treatment course. Since Rhonda's energy, concentration, and even interest in life were compromised, medication was a necessary first step. I started with an antidepressant. Then with brief psychotherapy, she was able to reconnect with herself and move beyond her pain. As in my experiences with Greg and Jake, the answers to the questions *What's wrong?* and *What must be done?* were clear in her initial visit.

WHAT DOES YOUR STORY TELL YOU?

Think about the lesson in the preceding cases. The first step in each of them involved listening carefully for diagnostic clues. For Greg to take charge, he needed to throw out an incorrect diagnosis. For Jake to heal, he needed to identify and treat an anxiety problem. For Rhonda to recover, she had to name and address her clinical depression.

To take charge of your emotional life, you'll need to consider the lessons of your own story. This starts with identifying your "presenting complaint," problem, distress, questions, and concerns. As you begin, consider the following questions:

- Might you meet the criteria for a diagnosis you haven't been given?

- Have you been tagged with a label that doesn't fit?

- Is it possible you have more than one condition?

- Are you carrying around ideas about who you are or what you ought to be doing that are a mismatch for your nature or essence as a human being?

- Is your "internal taskmaster" really a slave driver?

- Is your body trying to tell you something your brain doesn't want to accept?

- Are you sad, anxious, distractible, overwhelmed, irritable, forgetful, or highly sensitive to rejection and criticism? What's that all about?

In the following sections of this chapter, you'll find a series of questions and checklists drawn from my work with patients and the diagnostic criteria for common problems such as depression and anxiety. I urge you to answer these simple self-assessment queries. They'll help you determine whether a medical condition or chemical imbalance could be part of your presenting complaint or life problem.

But before beginning, let's talk about why you are the way you are and the importance of self-acceptance in healing.

THE ROOTS OF ILLNESS

In order to lay the proper foundation for healing, we need to explore questions such as *Do genes cause depression or attention deficit disorder (ADD)? What's the role of mind over matter?* and *Can we skip over the diagnostic piece and still heal?*

It turns out that we can receive a strong genetic vulnerability to illnesses such as depression, bipolar disorder, and panic attacks. So we are the way we are because of our ancestors . . . but genes aren't the whole story! Even identical twins aren't exactly the same. Although genetically identical twins are more likely to suffer from the same illnesses than even fraternal twins, no two individuals will have the exact same experience of well-being in their lives. Each of us is unique, and each life journey will be different.

Our genes play a huge role in what happens to us. They determine our vulnerability to disease in profound and powerful ways. Many illnesses, such as manic-depression and attention deficit disorder, run heavily along lines within families. However, gene expression is complex. It turns out that our experiences—even in utero—determine what, when, and how some of our genetic material appears later in life. Hence, even identical twins aren't carbon copies! There's a complicated interplay between our genetic endowment and what befalls us going forward, and the choices we make.

THE POWER OF CHOICE

We don't choose our vulnerability, and we can't control much of what affects our gene expression in the developmental years. What we *can* decide is whether or not we honor our nature and susceptibility, and how we respond to it.

For example, if you currently meet diagnostic criteria for major depression, generalized anxiety disorder, attention deficit disorder, or obsessive-compulsive disorder, you can choose to identify it and figure out what interventions to pursue. Think about Jake and Rhonda—naming their problems was the first step to taking charge of their emotional lives. Although you don't pick your disorders, you too can take charge of your life.

You can also decide what to tell yourself about your capability to heal; this is where mind-body techniques come into play. You have the ability to transform the trauma and challenge of just about anything you discover, if you honor and respond appropriately to your own story. But first you must identify *what is* in order to effect change. In giving voice and space to what exists now, you open the door to incredible growth and health.

Let's return to Maria and *The Sound of Music* for a moment. The tale wonderfully illustrates the power of self-acceptance in transforming lives. Remember the song that asks: "How do you solve a problem like Maria?" Mother Superior sings it when she discovers that Maria is late and unprepared for prayers again. The girl desperately wants to be a good nun, but she can't seem to get it right. Mother Superior describes the dilemma beautifully when she wonders how to catch a cloud, keep a wave in one place, or grasp a moonbeam.

Maria's brain isn't wired to be a nun. The structure doesn't suit her, so Mother Superior sends her off to be a governess. Identifying and respecting the young girl's true nature opened the door to what became a wondrous love and family life for her. If you want to be inspired to trust in the wisdom of your story and nature, see this film.

DISCOVER YOUR JOURNEY

I'd like you to start exploring *your* story by answering the questions that follow. You can learn amazing things about yourself when you take the time to visit your own history. In preparing for a first-time visit with me, many patients happen upon new insights. This week a new patient said, "I didn't realize until just last night that being diagnosed with cancer kept me from having time to grieve the loss of my father." What an important breakthrough that was!

In answering these inquiries about your own presenting problem, its history, and your nature, you may very well gain new insights. Be open to that possibility as you write down what comes to mind upon reading the ten questions below, and look for the lessons in your story.

1. What's bothering me? What's my presenting problem or chief complaint? Am I too anxious, self-critical, sad, angry, lonely, distractible, irritable, or hopeless (or some other state of being)?

2. What do I hope to change, accomplish, or transform with the Take-Charge program?

3. What's the story of my distress?
    - When did it start?
    - How has it shown itself over time?
    - What sort of interventions have I pursued?
    - What's been helpful?
    - What's made my problem worse?

4. When in my life have I felt my best?
    - Where was I?
    - How old was I?
    - How was I spending my time?

5. When have I felt my worst?
    - Where was I?
    - How old was I?
    - How was I spending my time?

6. What (or who) heals me, calms me, soothes me, and lifts my spirits?

7. What (or who) unsettles me, makes me sick, or makes me want to run for the hills?

8. If I could travel backward or forward from this point in the timeline of my life story, when would I visit and why?

9.   What's the role of my family history in my life and my problem?

10.   What, if anything, can I learn about my issue and my path to healing from my responses to these questions?

In answering these queries, you may have included experiences with psychiatric or medical conditions. Perhaps you wrote about problems with depression, anxiety, concentration, or memory. Maybe you noted a diagnosis (or several) that you've been given, or found yourself wondering if you have a condition that's been missed. You might even have been resistant to the idea of being diagnosed but realized that you need to consider its possibility.

HOW PSYCHIATRISTS DIAGNOSE DISORDERS

You might be wondering, *What does a "psychiatric" diagnosis really mean, anyway?* You may understand other kinds of illness (such as the medical condition of pneumonia) because you know you can see evidence of infection on a lung x-ray, but you may be confused about something like identifying major depression. Since you can't see anything in x-rays, and there's no blood test for it, you may find yourself questioning whether this is even a real illness.

This is a crucial question. The way diagnoses are made in psychiatry is on the basis of your story, not any laboratory test. If a person is suffering enough from a specific series of symptoms that the individual is unable to function, or he or she is overwhelmingly distressed by them, psychiatrists and medical doctors consider the person to have a *disorder* characterized by those symptoms. For example, someone with sleep and appetite disturbance, impaired memory and concentration, a lack of interest or pleasure in usual activities, or depressed mood and hopelessness would be considered to have the disorder of major depression.

How did that particular bunch of troubles get a specific name? Well, a group of experts actually meets periodically to determine what lists of symptoms should be classified as a disorder. They share their research and clinical-practice observations to reach a consensus on what makes sense. Then they publish their decisions in the *Diagnostic and Statistical Manual of Mental Disorders (DSM)*.

A new edition comes out every few years with changes that are the result of research and observations that have been gathered since the last publication. A different number is added to the end of the title to indicate what edition of criteria that book contains. The *DSM* is the bible of diagnosis in psychiatry, but unlike the real Bible, this work changes progressively over time.

Once diagnostic criteria are created, medication and treatment-intervention studies can be performed to see how to improve the symptoms of each disorder. This allows for the possibility of finding remedies and solutions. It also enables doctors, therapists, researchers, and patients to speak a common language and understand one another.

You see, although there's nothing absolute or magic about naming a series of symptoms of a disorder, doing so allows us to figure out how to help people move from a place of pain and hopelessness to a state of well-being. Over the years, we've learned that the vulnerability to groups of symptoms or conditions such as manic-depressive disorder, panic disorder, and attention deficit disorder are strongly genetically transmitted. We've also found that specific interventions can help heal those with these groups of symptoms—and that without those measures, some people won't get better.

You may have gotten stuck on your path to health because you lack a necessary diagnosis or carry one that doesn't fit. You may have received incorrect interventions or missed out on necessary ones. Like Greg, Jake, Rhonda, and Maria, you may be feeling lousy because you're going down the wrong path.

For this reason, it's really important to identify *what is*. You might consider:

- If you're sad or blue in a way that won't quit, you may be suffering from depression.

- If you're anxious, stressed out, or jumpy, you may have an anxiety disorder.

- If you're irritable or quick-tempered, you may be depressed, anxious, addicted, or have ADD.

- If you're forgetful or have trouble with memory and concentration, you may also be depressed, anxious, addicted, or be suffering from ADD.

- If your mood is erratic, with extreme highs and lows, you may have manic-depressive illness.

In order to help you determine whether you have a medical condition or a chemical imbalance, I've provided a series of questions for some of the most common problems people face. Although you'll find checklists for eight disorders, they cover three basic types of problems. The first two, depressive illness and bipolar disorder, are mood problems. The third through seventh—panic, obsessive-compulsive disorder, post-traumatic stress disorder, social phobia, and generalized anxiety disorder—are all anxiety disorders. And the eighth—attention deficit disorder—is a problem of memory, concentration, and impulsiveness.

Many of the checklists are drawn from National Institutes of Health (NIH) publications. The full text of these publications can be found at **www.nimh.nih.gov**. You can also find some of the information on my Website, **www.DrEveWood.com**; and in my first book, *There's Always Help; There's Always Hope,* where you'll find many examples of healing that illustrate the importance and method of making proper assessments, as well as stories that demonstrate how to include your diagnoses in a healing path that works.

COULD YOU BE SUFFERING FROM A DEPRESSIVE ILLNESS?

In any given one-year period, 9.5 percent of the population (or about 18.8 million Americans) suffer from a depressive illness. So when you attend a dinner party for ten people, at least one individual at the table will meet the criteria. In the supermarket when there are lines of six shoppers at eight checkout counters, at least six people in the front of the store are afflicted with depression. And the percentage is equally high in almost every other country in the world.

There are many kinds of depression. Some examples are major depressive disorder, seasonal affective disorder (SAD), dysthymia, and postpartum depression. To determine whether you could be suffering from a depressive illness, read through the following list of symptoms. Check off all the ones that you've experienced for at least two weeks:

DEPRESSION-SYMPTOM CHECKLIST

- ❏ A lasting sad, anxious, or empty mood
- ❏ Feelings of hopelessness or pessimism
- ❏ Feelings of guilt, worthlessness, or helplessness
- ❏ Loss of interest or pleasure in activities once enjoyed, including sex
- ❏ Decreased energy or a feeling of fatigue or of being "slowed down"
- ❏ Difficulty concentrating, remembering, or making decisions
- ❏ Restlessness or irritability
- ❏ Sleeping too much, or can't sleep
- ❏ Change in appetite and/or unintended weight loss or gain
- ❏ Chronic pain or other persistent bodily symptoms that aren't caused by physical illness or injury
- ❏ Thoughts of death or suicide, or suicide attempts

You may have a major depressive episode if you have five or more of these symptoms most of the day, nearly every day, for a period of two weeks or longer. But there's something surprising and crucial about this diagnosis: *You don't have to feel depressed in order to be suffering from such an illness!* You must have either a depressed mood *or* a loss of interest or pleasure in usual activities for two weeks to be considered clinically depressed. Often, sufferers don't feel sad or blue at all. They just don't care about anything—their usual passions seem irrelevant to them.

If you've put checks in five or more of the symptom boxes, you may well be suffering from a major depressive illness. If you checked at least three boxes, but fewer than five, you could be suffering from dysthymia, which is a chronic low-level depression that lasts for years.

If you have mood symptoms that occur only during the darker winter months, you could have SAD. If you're a woman who has recently given birth, you may be experiencing postpartum depression. Women are very vulnerable to developing depression immediately after giving birth. The abrupt drop in hormone levels during delivery, particularly estrogen, affects the brain.

If you've marked at least three of the symptom boxes and not been evaluated for depression by a doctor recently, I recommend that you schedule an assessment; you may well benefit from therapeutic intervention. This condition is quite treatable; but left untreated, it's second only to ischemic heart disease in the degree of morbidity and mortality that it causes in most countries in the world, for those over the age of five.

To learn more about depressive illness, visit:

- My Website: **www.DrEveWood.com** (click on "Medical Guidance")

- National Institute of Mental Health (NIMH): **www.nimh.nih.gov**

- National Alliance on Mental Illness (NAMI): **www.nami.org**

- International Foundation for Research and Education on Depression: **www.ifred.org**

COULD YOU BE SUFFERING FROM BIPOLAR DISORDER OR MANIC-DEPRESSIVE ILLNESS?

Bipolar disorder, also known as manic-depressive illness, affects more than two million American adults in any given year; it's equally common in many other countries. Bipolar disorder involves rapid mood swings—from overly "high" and/or irritable to sad and hopeless, and then back again. *Most* individuals with bipolar disorder are depressed for many more days of their life than they are "high" or manic.

To determine whether you could be suffering from bipolar disorder, check off all the symptoms of mania that you've experienced for one week or longer.

Manic-Episode Checklist

❑ Increased energy, activity, and restlessness

❑ Excessively "high," overly euphoric mood

❑ Extreme irritability

❑ Racing thoughts and talking very fast; jumping from one idea to another

❑ Distractibility, can't concentrate

❑ Little sleep needed

❑ Unrealistic beliefs in one's abilities and powers

❑ Poor judgment

❑ Spending sprees

❑ A lasting period of behavior that's different from the norm

❑ Increased sexual drive

❑ Abuse of drugs, particularly cocaine, alcohol, and sleep medications

❑ Provocative, intrusive, or aggressive behavior

❑ Denial that there's anything wrong

You might have had a manic episode if you experienced elevated mood with three or more of the other checklist symptoms for most of the day, nearly every day, for one week or longer. If your mood was irritable, you must have had four additional checklist symptoms for the episode to qualify.

In order to meet the criteria for manic-depressive illness, you would have to experience at least one episode of depressive illness *and* an episode of mania. If you checked off three or more boxes in the depression-symptom checklist and three or more in the manic-episode checklist, you could very well have bipolar disorder or cyclothymic disorder.

If you checked off two boxes in each list, you could have subthreshold bipolar disorder. It turns out that at least as many people suffer from this variation as meet the full criteria. These individuals have fewer checklist symptoms, but just as much impairment, in terms of the number of days a year (an average of 43) they're unable to work or perform normal daily activities.

Bipolar disorder, cyclothymic disorder, and subthreshold manic-depressive illness are all very treatable—and treatment is crucial. The risk of suicide in bipolar illness is much greater than in all other forms of depression. Even without this danger, the disease is often life crippling if sufferers don't receive adequate intervention. Medication is often necessary in the treatment of cyclical mood disorders, and it's best prescribed and monitored by a doctor familiar with these particular conditions.

If bipolar disorder, cyclothymia, or subthreshold bipolar disorder is a possibility for you, I recommend assessment by a psychiatrist, as opposed to any other medical doctor. Many primary-care physicians aren't knowledgeable enough to make these diagnoses.

For more information about bipolar and cyclical mood disorders, visit:

- My Website: **www.DrEveWood.com** (click on "Medical Guidance")

- National Institute of Mental Health (NIMH): **www.nimh.nih.gov**

- National Alliance on Mental Illness (NAMI): **www.nami.org**

- Depression and Bipolar Support Alliance: **www.DBSAlliance.org**

COULD YOU BE SUFFERING FROM A PANIC DISORDER?

In any given year, 2.4 million American adults will suffer from panic disorder; the frequency of this illness is similar in many other countries. People with this condition have feelings of terror that strike suddenly and repeatedly with no warning. They can't predict when an attack will occur, and many develop intense anxiety between episodes, worrying about when and where the next one will strike.

If you're having a panic attack, most likely your heart will pound; and you may feel sweaty, weak, faint, or dizzy. Your hands may tingle or feel numb, and you might be flushed or chilled. You may have nausea, chest pain, smothering sensations, a sense of unreality, or fear of impending doom or loss of control. You may genuinely believe that you're having a heart attack, losing your mind, or on the verge of death.

To determine whether you could be suffering from panic disorder, check off all the symptoms that you relate to in the following list. These must all occur during a sudden burst of fear that comes on for no apparent reason.

PANIC-DISORDER CHECKLIST

During sudden bursts of fear:
- ❑ I have chest pains or a racing heart.
- ❑ I have a hard time breathing or a choking feeling.
- ❑ I feel dizzy or sweat a lot.
- ❑ I have stomach problems or feel as if I need to throw up.
- ❑ I shake, tremble, or tingle.
- ❑ I feel out of control.
- ❑ I feel unreal.
- ❑ I'm afraid I'm dying or going crazy.

If you checked off three or more symptoms, you might be suffering from panic disorder. While an assessment can be done by most physicians, many can't provide the full course of treatment. Psychiatrists and many therapists, however, can do so. If medication is needed—and it often is, at least for a while—a psychiatrist or other medical doctor will need to prescribe it. A psychiatrist or other type of psychotherapist can often provide the rest of the treatment. Cognitive behavior therapy is an especially helpful approach for this condition.

My *Stop Anxiety Now Kit* (available in June 2007 through Hay House) is a good resource as well. It includes some mind-body techniques and cognitive-behavior tools, as well as a relaxation and guided-imagery CD to help you manage your anxiety.

For more information on panic disorder, visit:

- My Website: **www.DrEveWood.com** (click on "Medical Guidance")
- National Institute of Mental Health (NIMH): **www.nimh.nih.gov**
- National Alliance on Mental Illness (NAMI): **www.nami.org**
- Anxiety Disorders Association of America: **www.adaa.org**
- Freedom from Fear: **www.freedomfromfear.com**

COULD YOU BE SUFFERING FROM OBSESSIVE-COMPULSIVE DISORDER (OCD)?

In any given year, 3.3 million Americans will have OCD. If you do, you have repeated, upsetting thoughts. You do the same thing over and over again to make them go away, and you feel as if you can't control these thoughts or actions. Many people with OCD know that their behavior isn't normal, and they may to try to hide their problem from family and friends. Some sufferers may have trouble maintaining their jobs and relationships because of what they do.

If you have OCD, you feel trapped in a pattern of upsetting thoughts. To determine whether you might have this condition, check off all the symptoms that you relate to on the next page.

Obsessive-Compulsive Disorder Checklist

❑ Upsetting thoughts or images enter my mind again and again.

❑ I feel as if I can't stop these thoughts or images, even though I want to.

❑ I have a hard time stopping myself from doing things again and again, such as: counting, checking on things, washing my hands, rearranging objects, doing something until it feels right, or collecting useless objects.

❑ I worry a lot about terrible things that could happen if I'm not careful.

If you checked off two or more boxes, you could well have obsessive-compulsive disorder. Most psychologists and psychiatrists are equipped to evaluate you. Treatments include medication and cognitive behavioral therapy. For more information about OCD, visit:

- My Website: **www.DrEveWood.com** (click on "Medical Guidance")
- National Institute of Mental Health (NIMH): **www.nimh.nih.gov**
- National Alliance on Mental Illness (NAMI): **www.nami.org**
- Anxiety Disorders Association of America: **www.adaa.org**
- Obsessive Compulsive Foundation: **www.ocfoundation.org**

COULD YOU BE SUFFERING FROM POST-TRAUMATIC STRESS DISORDER?

In any given year, 5.2 million Americans have PTSD; this number is substantially higher in some countries where trauma and danger are a regular part of life. This debilitating condition can develop following a terrifying event. Often, sufferers have persistent frightening thoughts and memories of their ordeal and feel emotionally numb, especially with people they were once close to.

PTSD was first brought to public attention by war veterans, but it can result from any number of traumatic incidents. These include violent attacks such as mugging, rape, or torture; being kidnapped or held captive; child abuse; serious accidents such as car or train wrecks; and natural disasters such as floods or earthquakes. The triggering event may be something that threatened the person's life or that of someone close to him or her; or it could be something witnessed, such as massive death and destruction after a building is bombed or a plane crashes.

To determine whether you might have PTSD, consider your story. Have you lived through a scary and dangerous event? If so, review this checklist and mark all the symptoms you relate to.

Post-Traumatic Stress Disorder Checklist

❏   I feel as if the terrible event is happening all over again. This feeling often comes without warning.

❏   I have nightmares and scary memories of the terrifying event.

❏   I stay away from places that remind me of it.

❏   I jump and feel very upset when something happens without warning.

❏   I have a hard time trusting or feeling close to other people.

❏   I get mad very easily.

❏   I feel guilty because others died and I lived.

❏   I have trouble sleeping, and my muscles are tense.

If you marked three or more boxes in the PTSD checklist, you may have this condition.

Many therapists are equipped to make this diagnosis. Specific forms of psychotherapy and guided imagery are very helpful in the treatment of PTSD. A great resource for understanding trauma responses and how to heal is the book *Invisible Heroes: Survivors of Trauma and How They Heal* by Belleruth Naparstek. To learn more about this condition, visit:

- My Website: **www.DrEveWood.com** (click on "Medical Guidance")
- National Institute of Mental Health (NIMH): **www.nimh.nih.gov**
- Anxiety Disorders Association of America: **www.adaa.org**
- National Center for PTSD: **www.ncptsd.org**

COULD YOU BE SUFFERING FROM SOCIAL PHOBIA?

In any given year, at least 5.3 million Americans have this condition; the incidence is quite high in other countries as well. Social phobia, or social-anxiety disorder, involves overwhelming anxiety and excessive self-consciousness in everyday social situations. People with this illness have a persistent, intense, and chronic fear of being watched and judged by others and being embarrassed or humiliated by their own actions. Their terror may be so severe that it interferes with work, school, and other ordinary activities. While many sufferers recognize that their fear of being around others may be excessive or unreasonable, they're unable to overcome it. They often worry for days or weeks in advance of a dreaded situation.

If you feel afraid and uncomfortable when you're around other people, you could have social phobia. Please review the checklist and mark all the statements that you relate to.

Social-Phobia Checklist

❑ I have an intense fear that I'll do or say something to embarrass myself in front of other people.

❑ I'm always very afraid of making a mistake and being watched and judged.

❑ My fear of embarrassment makes me avoid doing things I want to do or speaking to others.

❑ I worry for days or weeks before I have to meet new people.

❑ I blush, sweat a lot, tremble, or feel like I have to throw up before and during an event where I am with anyone I don't know.

❑ I usually stay away from social situations such as school events and making speeches.

❑ I often drink to try to make these fears go away.

If you marked three or more boxes in the social-phobia checklist, you may have this condition. Many therapists, psychologists, and psychiatrists are equipped to make this diagnosis; generally, internists are not. Treatments can include medication, psychotherapy, and cognitive-behavioral interventions.

For more information about social phobia, visit:

- My Website: **www.DrEveWood.com** (click on "Medical Guidance")
- National Alliance on Mental Illness (NAMI): **www.nami.org**
- Anxiety Disorders Association of America: **www.adaa.org**

COULD YOU HAVE GENERALIZED ANXIETY DISORDER (GAD)?

In any given year, four million Americans will have GAD; the disorder is common in many other countries. If you have this condition, you worry all the time about your family, health, or work, even when there are no signs of trouble. Sometimes you aren't anxious about anything special, but still feel tense and nervous all day long. You also have aches and pains for no reason and feel tired a lot. Everyone gets worried sometimes, but if you have GAD, you stay that way, fear the worst will happen, and can't relax.

If you worry almost all the time, you may have GAD. To determine the likelihood, please check off the statements that are true for you:

GENERALIZED-ANXIETY-DISORDER CHECKLIST

❑   I never stop worrying about things big and small.

❑   I have headaches and other aches and pains for no reason.

❑   I'm tense a lot and have difficulty relaxing.

❑   I have trouble keeping my mind on one thing.

❑   I get crabby or grouchy. I have a hard time falling asleep or staying asleep.

❑   I sweat and have hot flashes.

❑   I sometimes have a lump in my throat or feel that I need to throw up when I'm worried.

If you put a check next to three or more of the above statements, you may have GAD. Most therapists, psychologists, and psychiatrists can make this diagnosis, but many internists miss it when patients come in with a series of physical complaints. Remember, this was Jake's story. Treatment often involves medication, and some additional form of therapy. My *Stop Anxiety Now Kit* (available June 2007 from Hay House) can help you manage the anxiety of GAD.

For more information, visit:

- My Website: **www.DrEveWood.com** (click on "Medical Guidance")

- National Institute of Mental Health (NIMH): **www.nimh.nih.gov**

- Anxiety Disorders Association of America: **www.adaa.org**

COULD YOU HAVE ATTENTION DEFICIT DISORDER?

At least two million adults in the United States suffer from attention deficit disorder (ADD), also known as attention-deficit/hyperactivity disorder (ADHD); it's common in other countries as well. By definition, the problem has to begin early in life, before age seven, and continue for at least six months. Although many adults who have recently been identified as having ADHD weren't diagnosed when they were young, their childhood stories have to fit the criteria. *Some* symptoms must have been present before the age of seven.

At present, ADHD is a diagnosis applied to children and adults who consistently display certain characteristic behaviors over a period of time. The most common actions fall into three categories:

1. **Inattention.** People who are inattentive have a hard time keeping their mind on any one thing and may get bored with a task after only a few minutes. They may give effortless, automatic consideration to activities and things they enjoy. But focusing deliberate, conscious attention on organizing and completing a task or learning something new is difficult.

2. **Hyperactivity.** People who are hyperactive always seem to be in motion. They can't keep still, so they may dash around or talk incessantly. Sitting through a lesson can be an impossible task. Hyperactive children squirm in their seats or roam around the room; or they might wiggle their feet, touch everything, or noisily tap their pencils. Teens and adults can feel intensely restless. They may be fidgety or try to do several things at once, bouncing around from one activity to the next.

3. **Impulsivity.** People who are overly impulsive seem unable to curb their immediate reactions or think before they act. As a result, they may blurt out inappropriate comments. Children may run into the street without looking. Their impulsivity may make it hard for them to wait for things they want or to take their turn in games.

Not everyone who's overly hyperactive, inattentive, or impulsive has an attention disorder. Since most people sometimes blurt out things they didn't mean to say, bounce from one task to another, or become disorganized and forgetful, how can specialists tell if the problem is ADHD?

To assess this condition, we consider several critical questions:

- Are these behaviors excessive, long-term, and pervasive? That is, do they occur more often than in other people the same age?

- Are the issues a continual problem, not just a response to a temporary situation?

- Do the behaviors occur in several settings or only in one specific place, such as the playground or the office?

The pattern of behavior is compared against a set of criteria and characteristics of the disorder, which appear in the DSM. According to the manual, there are three patterns of behavior that indicate ADHD: Sufferers may show several signs of being consistently inattentive, have a pattern of being hyperactive or impulsive, or they may show all three types of behavior.

In order to determine whether or not you could be suffering from ADHD, check off as many symptom statements as you relate to in the following list. Some of the characteristics must be present in more than one setting.

Attention-Deficit/Hyperactivity Disorder Checklist

Inattention

❑   I make careless mistakes in work or during other activities.

❑   It's hard for me to pay attention while reading or sitting in a meeting.

❑   I have trouble following through, completing assignments or tasks.

❑   I have difficulty getting organized.

❑   I avoid activities that require concentration for very long.

❑   I continually lose what I need, such as keys, pens, books, and tools.

❑   I'm easily distracted.

❑   I'm forgetful.

Hyperactive/Impulsive

❑   I feel restless when I have to sit still.

❑   I have trouble amusing myself quietly.

❑   I'm always on the go.

❑   I talk excessively.

❑   I interrupt often.

❑   I have a hard time waiting in line, in traffic, or for my turn in other situations.

❑   I answer questions before they're completed.

If you checked off four boxes in either the Inattention or Hyperactive/Impulsive sections, you could very well have ADD or ADHD. You may be suffering with this disorder even if you're a highly successful professional. I've treated many physicians and attorneys with this problem. In *There's Always Help; There's Always Hope,* you'll find lots of examples of gifted individuals who were held back by their undiagnosed ADD.

If this condition is a possibility for you, begin to educate yourself about the disorder. There are many great books and resources out there. One of my favorite books for this is *Driven to Distraction* by Edward M. Hallowell, M.D., and John J. Ratey, M.D. While many professionals can help you make this diagnosis, you can sort out its likelihood very well on your own first.

Interventions range from medication, coaching, and time-management techniques to psychotherapy. To learn more about ADD/ADHD visit:

- My Website: **www.DrEveWood.com** (click on "Medical Guidance")
- A.D.D WareHouse: **www.addwarehouse.com**
- Children and Adults with Attention-Deficit/Hyperactivity Disorder: **www.chadd.org**
- National Institute of Mental Health (NIMH): **www.nimh.nih.gov**

You've come to the end of the checklists for common disorders. Take a few moments to make note of what you've discovered. Did something important jump out at you or surprise you? Is there something you need to pursue?

If you related to one or more of the conditions described, you're not alone. Take the lesson seriously. According to the *Archives of General Psychiatry* (June 2005), 55 percent of Americans will suffer from a mental illness in their lifetime. The breakdown of most types is given in the chart on the next page. Please note that the general numbers (such as 28.8 percent for any anxiety disorder) indicate the percentage of the 55 percent of Americans just mentioned who experience the condition. The specific percentages (such as panic disorder, agoraphobia without panic, and so on) may add up to more than the general number because many individuals are diagnosed with more than one condition.

ANY ANXIETY DISORDER	28.8%
Panic disorder	4.7%
Agoraphobia without panic	1.4%
Specific phobia	12.5%
Social phobia	12.1%
Generalized anxiety disorder	5.7%
Post-traumatic stress disorder	6.8%
Obsessive-compulsive disorder	1.6%
Separation anxiety	5.2%
MOOD DISORDER	20.8%
Major depression	16.6%
Dysthymia	2.5%
Bipolar I or II	3.9%
IMPULSE-CONTROL DISORDER	24.8%
Oppositional-defiant disorder	8.5%
Conduct disorder	9.5%
Attention-deficit/hyperactivity disorder	8.1%
Intermittent explosive disorder	5.2%
SUBSTANCE DISORDER	14.6%
Alcohol abuse	13.6%
Alcohol dependence	5.4%
Drug abuse	7.9%
Drug dependence	3%

While I didn't provide you checklists for every disorder on the list, you'll notice that the anxiety, mood, and attention-related conditions are the most common problems. I chose not to include the other big category—alcoholism and other addictions—in this book because there are many resources that cover these problems quite well.

Given how common substance use and abuse is, you may have problems in this area. If so, please pursue appropriate treatment and support. I love the 12-step recovery programs such as AA (Alcoholics Anonymous), NA (Narcotics Anonymous), SLAA (Sex and Love Addicts Anonymous), and OA (Overeaters Anonymous) for the support and guidance they provide.

For more information on addictions, visit:

The 12-step recovery programs:

- AA (Alcoholics Anonymous): **www.alcoholics-anonymous.org**

- NA (Narcotics Anonymous): **www.na.org**

- SLAA (Sex and Love Addiction Anonymous): **www.slaafws.org**

- OA (Overeaters Anonymous): **www.oa.org**

- GA (Gamblers Anonymous): **www.gamblersanonymous.org**

- DA (Debtors Anonymous): **www.debtorsanonymous.org**

- Al-Anon/Alateen: **www.al-anon.alateen.org**

Additional resources:

- National Council on Alcoholism and Drug Dependence: **www.ncadd.org**

- National Institute on Alcohol Abuse and Alcoholism: **www.niaaa.nih.gov**

In Step 1, you've explored the lessons within your story and have considered the possibility that you may have diagnoses requiring attention. As you now know, the ultimate determinant of whether you meet criteria for a disorder is whether your symptoms match those in the *DSM* (*DSM-IV-R*, as of this printing). While I could not possibly reprint the whole manual, you can find it in your local library or bookstore and compare your symptoms with those of any disorder that you sense could fit.

If your story matches completely, you know you meet the criteria; if it doesn't, you don't. You can figure out a lot for yourself. In fact, I often share the criteria with my patients to be sure that we're on the same diagnostic page. The information isn't that tough to understand. It's easily accessible and the gold standard when it comes to making a psychiatric diagnosis.

Before moving on, I need to make a plug for a particular type of medical assessment. I want you to be open to the possibility that you could need an evaluation of your general health, because it turns out that there are quite a few general medical conditions that can look like psychiatric problems even though they're not.

For example, if you have an underactive thyroid, you may feel like a person with major depression. By contrast, if you have an overactive thyroid, you might feel as though you have an anxiety disorder. Minor and easily treated medical problems like vitamin-B_{12} deficiency and thyroid abnormalities can also masquerade as mental illnesses. Occasionally, serious but very rare problems such as brain tumors and autoimmune diseases can appear to be psychiatric problems as well. Finally, many hormonal shifts, such as those that occur during perimenopause and menopause, can wreck havoc on the emotional brain.

So if your symptoms don't completely fit *DSM* criteria, or if you don't respond to the usual treatment interventions, something else could be going on. In that case, I recommend a general-health assessment with your internist, family practitioner, or gynecologist.

Before closing this chapter, I want to review a point we visited earlier on: *You don't choose your vulnerabilities or diagnoses. You only decide whether you identify and address them.* As we finish Step 1, please answer the following questions:

1. What have I identified (diagnoses, etc.)?
2. How do I want to address what I've found up to this point?
3. What are the lessons of my story?

As you move on to Step 2 in the next chapter, you'll begin to explore your need for medication. If you have clinical depression, an anxiety disorder, or ADD, medication *may* be part of your answer—and then again, it *may* not. There's no "one-size-fits-all" answer in the Take-Charge program. Your story and needs are unique, and your personal path is waiting for you. With enough information and support, your inner wisdom will guide you to your own best solutions. You can take charge, and you *can* heal!

STEP 2

Explore Your Need for Medication

Welcome to Step 2 of the program! In Step 1 you examined your story and looked for its lessons, exploring the question *Do I have a medical condition or clinical diagnosis?* In reviewing the checklists, you may have identified one or more disorders that could explain part of your struggle; or you may have discovered that a diagnosis you've been given doesn't fit your story.

In Step 2, you'll explore your need for medication, which is a mixed bag. Many lives have been transformed for good with this type of intervention—in fact, lots of people say, "Medication saved my life." But there are other voices out there, too, and some individuals blame drugs for actual deaths. The FDA has issued warnings about the possibility of increased suicide risk with the use of some prescriptions. We're entering an area of controversy and confusion as we begin Step 2 together.

But you don't need to get confused or overwhelmed by this issue, because I'll help you find your way through the labyrinth. You'll discover how to learn your own personal answer to the question *What's the place of medication in my journey?* There are four specific principles to consider in evaluating this, but first I need to give you some background.

Shakespeare wrote: "There is nothing either good or bad but thinking makes it so." Those who tell you that medication is all positive or completely negative are misguided in their thinking. Unfortunately, you're regularly exposed to extreme messages from both camps: champions and critics of this treatment option.

In reality, a particular prescription might be great for you, or it might be terrible; a drug may save your life or disrupt it. You might benefit for a brief period or need ongoing assistance. You may be tipped into your first manic episode by an antidepressant or experience unbearable side effects. Sometimes medicine is good and sometimes it isn't—it all depends on the situation. Your need is related to your vulnerability, your challenges, and your unique tale.

As you know, we're all born with different degrees of susceptibility to illnesses and disorders, which continue to be affected by our developmental and life experiences. Given our family histories, genetics, and particular challenges, some of us are much more prone to becoming clinically depressed, anxious, or addicted than others. With enough stress and loss, most of us will become depressed, worried, or overwhelmed, but our individual tolerance points are very different.

For example, I come from a family with strong genetic loading for clinical depression. Both my maternal grandfather and my mother took antidepressant medication for years to control insomnia, hopelessness, fearfulness, and negativity. Neither was particularly interested in, or inclined to do, much else that might have lifted their moods. But even had they chosen to do more, it might not have made a difference. On my dad's side of the family, I have some genetic loading for alcoholism. That wasn't in a first-degree relative, so it may not be as strong.

In any case, I've never yet experienced a full-blown clinical depression that required medication. But I surely could, and I'd take pills if I needed them to heal. And although I've never suffered from this condition, I can get down or blue if I stop my regular self-care regimen. I do a lot of things that are felt to be protective; several have even been shown to be natural antidepressants *for some people.* I exercise aerobically for at least 30 minutes five days a week. I sing, pray, attend religious services weekly, maintain ongoing social connections, see patients, teach, and give back in many other ways. I spend time outdoors under the Tucson, Arizona, sun daily (except when traveling);

write books and articles to foster personal empowerment and health; nurture the growth of my four children; and make time for fun with my kids, friends, and soul-mate husband.

As you can tell, I'm a super-busy lady who's juggling and balancing a lot, and as a result, I regularly do a bunch of things that decrease my vulnerability to illness. You'll learn more about those interventions in subsequent chapters. Because of my good fortune, genetic endowment, attitude, and life choices, I'm usually upbeat and hopeful. However, when I get thrown too many curveballs, my system can get overwhelmed, and I sometimes feel pretty anxious.

On rare occasions, I become so unsettled that I can't calm down enough to sleep at night. When that happens, I take a tiny dose of Valium; one milligram is usually enough to turn my system around. I may need to take a pill as often as once every three months. Whenever I do this, it interrupts my anxiety, and by the next day, I head for the gym first thing in the morning and am lucky enough to be back to feeling like myself again before breakfast. That's my story. I happen to be very resilient, and my dad was the same way. But you have your own history, endowment, and vulnerabilities. You may be like me, or you may be more like my mom and grandpa. You might not even be like any of us, because ultimately, you're just *you* . . . and it's *your* story that counts.

Pamela's story and Christina's tale are two more examples that illustrate how individual differences dictate the need for medication in the Take-Charge program. You might see the former as one side of the coin and the latter as the other, but it isn't so black and white. See what you think. . . .

Help along the Path: Pamela's Story

Pamela, a bubbly woman in her 50s, was referred to me by several close friends who were worried about her. Her husband of many years was dying of cancer, and she was quite overwhelmed and anxious—just not herself. She told me how grateful she was for the referral as she settled into a seat in my office for the first time.

Pamela hadn't been in therapy before and had never been evaluated by a psychiatrist. As she told me her story, I determined that she was suffering from what *DSM* calls an "adjustment disorder with anxious mood." That basically means that she was struggling with unsettlement caused by significant life stress. She didn't meet diagnostic criteria for an anxiety disorder, depressive illness, or anything additional. She needed supportive psychotherapy and practical guidance, yet her internist had started her on an antidepressant several weeks before.

I questioned her about his rationale. "Why did he put you on this medicine?" I asked.

"Well," she said, "I'm not sure. I told him that I wasn't sleeping and needed something for it. Was that a poor choice?"

Together we explored her story and determined that the antidepressant might not have been the best idea. However, since her husband was dying, she was at a higher risk than normal for developing an anxiety or depressive disorder. Because she was already feeling somewhat overwhelmed and wasn't having any problem with the drug, we decided not to stop it right away. Although I probably wouldn't have started it initially, I was concerned about ceasing the medication at such a challenging time in her life—after all, perhaps it was helping her somewhat. What if she were to become worse off without it? It made sense to continue her prescription for the time being.

Pamela and I met for several months as I helped her through the death of her husband and the grieving and rebuilding process that followed. She did extremely well through the whole ordeal. She then chose to taper off the medication after a total of six months from the original start date. This felt completely appropriate to me, and she did quite well thereafter.

An Ongoing Experience: Christina's Story

Christina, a 32-year-old graduate student, wasn't feeling very well: She was "down in the dumps" again. During her first appointment, she told me that at the suggestion of several health practitioners, she'd cut down her antidepressant dose during the prior week. Concerned about this decision and its aftermath, I asked Christina to tell me her story. Why was she on the drug in the first place, and how had it helped her?

It turned out that she'd been suffering from depressive illness since childhood. She'd been in and out of therapy over the years and had been repeatedly suicidal. Although she'd come quite close several times, she'd never made a suicide attempt. Medication had always managed to lift her depression. She'd been on it for a long time, yet she'd periodically find herself thinking that she ought to be okay without it, and that taking the pills was some sort of weakness. She'd then start cutting down on them. Invariably, she'd get depressed, and sometimes even suicidal, before resuming a therapeutic dose of the drug.

Christina had a very strong family history of mental illness as well. She told me that many of her relatives over several generations were known to have suffered from clinical depression. In fact, several close family members had committed suicide. There was a lot of psychosis, addiction, depression, and anxiety in her siblings, parents, cousins, aunts, and uncles.

My patient shared all of this information in a very matter-of-fact way; she seemed totally detached from its significance. She told me that no matter what her family history was, she ought to be able to handle her moods without medication. She was unrelenting in her self-criticism, and unrealistic in what she expected of herself.

In dealing with this situation, I needed to take a completely different position than I did in helping Pamela. I explained to Christina that she had a life-threatening, recurring illness that was beyond her control. For her, as for so many other people, depression was a chronic condition that could worsen over time. The vulnerability to this runs in families, and her genetic loading was very strong.

For individuals like herself who've suffered from at least two depressive episodes, the likelihood of an additional one is above 90 percent. She was at high risk for recurrence and suicide, so she needed to increase her antidepressant dose right away. I explained that taking medication might be an ongoing part of her life, and that acceptance of *what is* was going to be a big piece of her therapeutic work.

Although she was disappointed, Christina did as I suggested. She resumed her usual drug regimen and reported feeling more hopeful and energized by the next time we got together. Thankfully, she responded quickly to the dosage increase.

⸙

Before you read on, take a moment to reflect on these stories. Do you relate to my experience, Pamela's or Christina's story, or bits of each? Do you recognize that these three situations cover a spectrum of vulnerability and need? Perhaps you realize that so far, medication is *mostly unnecessary* for me, might have been *briefly necessary* for Pamela, and is *absolutely crucial* for Christina in an ongoing way.

Remember the enduring lesson from Step 1: The answer to the question *What's wrong with the patient and what must be done to promote healing?* is in the presenting complaint and the initial clinical history. Your need for medication depends on your background, unique vulnerability, and personal story.

THE FOUR PRINCIPLES

Earlier in this chapter, I said that there are four specific principles you could use to figure out whether you need to take medication as part of your Take-Charge program. In this section, I'll teach them to you and show you how to use them to evaluate yourself. As I explain the principles, I'll share some clinical examples and give you guidance on how to work with each one. Then in Step 3, we'll explore *how* to use pharmaceuticals in treating depression, anxiety, ADD, and nonspecific problems that fall outside of the diagnostic categories. By the end of the next chapter, you'll have a good idea of whether this treatment is an option, possibility, or necessity for you, and also how to use it.

Medication only makes sense and may be necessary when:

1. You've identified a specific problem or diagnosis.

2. You've established target symptoms.

3. A specific medication has been shown to relieve the identified target symptoms of your specific problem.

4. The risks of you taking that medication outweigh the risks of avoiding it.

These four principles are crucial to your success in the Take-Charge program. If you get them down pat and live by them, you'll transform your life. If you neglect them, you may very well find yourself overwhelmed and spinning out of control for a long time.

PRINCIPLE 1: MEDICATION ONLY MAKES SENSE AND MAY BE NECESSARY WHEN YOU'VE IDENTIFIED A SPECIFIC PROBLEM OR DIAGNOSIS

This is a basic concept: We doctors should not treat a set of symptoms without determining the actual cause behind them. And you, as the sufferer, shouldn't take prescription medication if you don't know or understand why it's being given to you.

Why is it important to identify your diagnosis or problem? Remember what you learned in Step 1: In giving a set of symptoms a name, or diagnostic label, we can begin to figure out what treatment interventions work. Our medications have only been studied and shown to be effective for specific disorders. If you take a drug but don't have any symptoms that have been shown to respond to that substance, there's a good chance that you won't be helped by it. You might even get derailed or suffer unnecessarily.

We need to know what we're treating; we have to figure out *what is*. When we use medication indiscriminately, we can make actual conditions worse. We can end up on the wrong path or even create brand new problems. All drugs have side effects. The last thing you need to experience when you're already distressed is a series of unpleasant or troubling symptoms from a medication you don't even need, so let's look at some examples of problematic and effective medicine use.

Do you remember Jake's story? When he came to me, he was being treated for back pain with a bunch of powerful medications. His suffering had been getting worse and worse over the course of three years, and the prescriptions were doing little to make his life work, as he was spending more and more time in bed. But his discomfort was the result of an undiagnosed, and of course, untreated, generalized anxiety disorder. Once we made the proper assessment together, Jake began appropriate medication (a long-acting antianxiety agent) and psychotherapy. He improved and was thus able to move on with his life.

What's the lesson? A faulty diagnosis led to the wrong medication and progressive deterioration; the right knowledge and correct drug opened the door to healing.

Recall the details of Pamela's situation: Her internist started her on an antidepressant when she was complaining of insomnia. Luckily, she tolerated the substance well and didn't suffer from side effects. But because it wasn't clear whether the substance was needed in the first place, we were reluctant to stop it for a while. Had she clearly met the criteria for depression or anxiety in the internist's office, and had she understood the diagnosis and need for treatment, she and I would have known that it was important to continue her prescription for six months to a year. What's the lesson? The confusion about the reason for starting the medication made it difficult to know whether it could be stopped; clarity would have determined the right path.

There's another crucial lesson to be learned from Pamela's story. Today, antidepressants are among the most commonly consumed medications in the world. Most prescriptions for these drugs are written by internists and primary-care physicians. Unfortunately, many doctors don't focus on making a diagnosis before prescribing these pills. Therefore, lots of people who are taking them don't know why. Some probably don't need them and shouldn't be on them!

Please don't begin taking prescription medications before you understand why you may need them, and don't stop taking a drug until you know it makes sense to do so. Ask your physician to explain her rationale for the treatment recommendation, and make sure you agree. Don't assume that a doctor knows best and you have nothing to contribute to the discussion. You *can* take charge of your emotional health, so expect to partner with your care provider. Speak up! Your inner wisdom is brilliant and may recognize a bad fit between the official assessment and your story. You know yourself a whole lot better than anyone else does, so you're uniquely suited to identify mismatches and proper fits.

Another aspect of the first principle is that *medication only makes sense, and may be <u>necessary</u>, when you have identified a specific problem.* Think about Christina's story in light of this principle, and focus on the word *necessary.* Remember, Christina met diagnostic criteria for recurrent major depression. Her diagnosis, scary family history of suicides, and ongoing experiences of suicidal thoughts made medication a necessity in her Take-Charge program. Nothing else had ever worked to transform her hopelessness and devastation, and with untreated depression, she was at high risk for suicide. The diagnosis dictated the medication choice, while the family history and personal story demonstrated the necessity of treatment.

Now that you have clarity about the importance of making a diagnosis before beginning drug therapy, let's move on to the next principle.

PRINCIPLE 2: MEDICATION ONLY MAKES SENSE AND MAY BE NECESSARY WHEN YOU'VE IDENTIFIED TARGET SYMPTOMS

You're probably wondering what these symptoms are. *Target* is a strange word to use when talking about healing, since it seems sort of aggressive. But if you conjure up the image of a target in your mind and begin to visualize yourself shooting arrows or darts in the hopes of hitting a bull's-eye, you'll make the connection. You see, the target represents the set of symptoms you're trying to treat with your "arrows" or therapeutic interventions.

Just as it is dangerous and pointless to shoot arrows into thin air, it's wasteful and potentially harmful to take medication if we haven't identified specific symptoms that we hope to improve or make better with the drug. Furthermore, without identifying and examining these target symptoms over time, we have no way to evaluate whether a drug or medication is working.

Let's look at an example to clarify this concept. Think back to Rhonda's story and what happened after her house was burglarized. She said:

- I can't get my work done.
- I can't concentrate.
- I don't care about what used to matter to me.
- Food doesn't interest me.
- I cry all the time.
- I wish I could go to sleep and not wake up.
- Life feels pointless.
- I don't feel like myself.

This list of problems helped me ascertain that Rhonda was suffering from a clinical depression. However, they also had another use. I made these statements the target symptoms, the specific issues, that I hoped to see improve once Rhonda began taking antidepressant medication.

Week by week, the two of us would look at shifts in these troubles. How would we evaluate change? We set up a rating system. The scale went from 1 to 10, where 1 was *not at all or never,* and 10 was *almost always.* I asked Rhonda to rate each statement before we started medication; each symptom was rated a 10 or almost always. Week by week, she categorized her symptoms. As time went on, the numbers got lower, indicating that the drug was working.

You might question why a rating scale and list of target symptoms is necessary. Perhaps you're saying to yourself, *I'd know if I were getting better. It would be obvious.* Although that idea may make sense to you, the reality is that it doesn't work that way. Quite often, the last target symptom to improve is the depressed, anxious, or hopeless mood. Your sleep, concentration, and energy level may change dramatically before you *feel* better. Without some way to document that the other symptoms are improving, people who are getting better may insist that nothing is changing. This tool can help you maintain perspective and stay with the program.

The list can also enable you to realize when treatment *isn't* working. If your list of troubles is unchanged in spite of intervention, you'll realize your need to switch to another medication or change course in some other way.

I don't know how I'd judge the success of any therapeutic intervention without using target symptoms. Remember, Principle 1 involves identifying the diagnosis or problem clearly before intervening; this is a crucial first step. But how do we get involved and ensure success? We need to identify our goals and use a rating scale. Without a specific list of day-to-day, nuts-and-bolts troubles to follow, we have no way of evaluating the benefit of any treatment.

As part of your Take-Charge program, you'll need to create a list of the target symptoms you hope to improve. This exercise is crucial, whether you pursue medication intervention or any other step we'll be covering. Not only will you need to know *what is* (the problem and the diagnosis) in order to take charge, you'll also have to track *how it is* (day-to-day struggles), too.

How do you create your list of target symptoms? Well, you can start by using the checklists in Step 1. If you related to any of the disorders there, you can use the statements you checked off. I suggest that you take some time to note your target symptoms before moving on to the third principle. Feel free to write your day-to-day difficulties on the lines provided here or on a separate piece of paper.

My List of Target Symptoms

The day-to-day difficulties I want to heal:

1. _____
2. _____
3. _____
4. _____
5. _____
6. _____
7. _____
8. _____
9. _____
10. _____

I've also provided a rating scale so that you can assess your progress. I suggest making additional copies of it so that you can keep using it over time. It can help you evaluate your improvement with medication, as well as with many of the other self-care and treatment interventions that we'll be discussing in later steps or chapters.

Please don't chart your progress more often than once per week. No change happens faster than that, and many improvements are much longer in coming.

My Progress: Rating Scale

Use a scale from 1 to 10, where **1 = Almost Never,** and **10 = Always.**

SYMPTOMS	Date: / /	Date: / /	Date: / /	Date: / /	Date: / /
	Rating	Rating	Rating	Rating	Rating
1.					
2.					
3.					
4.					
5.					

Principle 3: Medication Only Makes Sense and May Be Necessary When That Specific Drug Has Been Shown (or Proven in Clinical Studies) to Relieve the Identified Target Symptoms of the Specific Problem

Once you make a diagnosis and create a specific target-symptom list, the medication that you choose should be known to make your diagnosis and set of day-to-day troubles better. If you use a drug to treat a problem that it isn't known to improve, it probably won't help—and it may even make matters worse.

Let me give you an example of what I mean here. Daniel came to me with panic attacks, a type of anxiety disorder. Although he had attacks about once or twice a week, which would come on abruptly and last about 15 minutes, he'd been prescribed an anti-anxiety medication that takes more than 30 minutes to begin to work and lasts for eight to ten hours. Since the drug wasn't acting quickly enough, he was getting worse over time. And since he was taking something that lasted longer than he needed, he felt drowsy and depressed for hours after swallowing each pill.

This medication *has* been found to be useful in GAD. In fact, it's what I prescribed for Jake (the anxious man with headaches). It worked well for him because he was anxious all the time. However, it was a very poor choice for Daniel, who needed medication that was quick to take effect and short term. He should have something that he could use whenever he began to feel a panic attack coming on. When I switched him to one of those fast, short-acting drugs—one that's been shown to be effective in treating the target symptoms of panic disorder—he improved immediately.

As you take charge of your emotional health, I want you to find out how any medication you're taking or considering is used to treat your diagnosis and target symptoms. Ask your treatment provider, "Has this been shown to help my type of problem?" Be sure you understand what you should expect from the prescription and that you know how to use it, because if you don't take it in the way it's been shown to be helpful, it won't work.

For example, Daniel needed to use the short-acting anti-anxiety drug I prescribed as soon as he began to feel anxious or sense that a panic attack could be coming on. This technique is what works to stop escalating worry. If the anxiety continued to increase for more than 20 minutes, he was to take a second pill. This step-by-step approach has been shown to interrupt the cycle.

Jake, on the other hand, was to take his long-acting medication every morning, afternoon, and evening. He needed to adjust the dose according to his level of anxiety at the time. This method works for GAD.

As you take charge of your emotional life, be sure you identify your diagnoses (if any), target symptoms, and the role medication can play in addressing your particular problem and day-to-day difficulties. Before we move on to the fourth principle, I encourage you to reflect on how the third one applies to your story.

If you're on medication or considering a particular drug, is it a suitable fit? Has it been shown to help your problem and its symptoms? Do you know how to take the drug in the proper way? Are you able to work with your treatment provider to answer these questions? If the answer to the last question is no, I urge you to find a suitable partner before going much further. In the Take-Charge program, you must always choose professional relationships that are good fits for you. You deserve to have what works, and you can find it!

PRINCIPLE 4: MEDICATION ONLY MAKES SENSE AND MAY BE NECESSARY WHEN THE RISKS OF AVOIDING IT OUTWEIGH THE RISKS OF TAKING IT

We can think about this principle as the risk-benefit consideration. Each drug has potential risks or side effects, as well as possible benefits or healing results. Think about Daniel with panic attacks and Jake with generalized anxiety disorder for a moment. The same long-acting anti-anxiety prescription had more risk than benefit for the former patient, but vice versa for the latter—in other words, Daniel got worse on it, while Jake got better.

Each illness, disorder, problem, and diagnosed condition poses a certain degree of risk to your life and well-being when untreated, and offers benefits if treated. For example, Christina's recurring episodes of major depression and ongoing suicidal thoughts meant that she was at high risk for death without treatment. Although she was reluctant to take an antidepressant, she tolerated it with few problems and experienced dramatic improvement.

Every medication that's available has been studied, and shown to offer some value in addressing some sort of problem, and every single drug has hundreds of possible side effects. Some people are extremely responsive to the benefits and experience few side effects, while others are quite sensitive and have more difficulty finding drugs that work without causing undue distress. No person is equally responsive to the ups and downs of all medicines, since every agent acts and is metabolized differently in the body. There's no way to predict your reaction, so finding the right drug to treat your anxiety, depression, or ADD will always involve some trial and error.

A particular medication may help you somewhat, but not enough. It may cause you to be less anxious or depressed—for example, taking your target symptoms from a level 10 to a level 5. This suboptimal response may be the result of an inadequate dose. If so, increasing the amount you're consuming will also up your benefit. Or it could be that you're experiencing a partial response to the maximum suggested dose, which isn't unusual.

We often need to switch drugs or include additional ones. Furthermore, most medications are only one piece of the treatment puzzle.

We routinely need to add other interventions to our Take-Charge programs, and we'll visit these complementary steps in subsequent chapters. In the meantime, let's summarize and take stock of where we are so far.

REVIEW YOUR STORY AND THE POSSIBILITY OF MEDICATION

By now, you know that taking medication is a mixed bag: It can help and harm. Your life can be transformed with pharmacological intervention, and this step might even be the door to your future! Adding a proper chemical adjustment to your system may be the first and most crucial action you'll take in this program, but how can you know what you ought to do? What are the risk-benefit issues related to medicine in your story?

I want you to begin to think about your problems, your diagnoses, and your level of distress. You, and only you, are inside your body, living your life day after day. You're the only one who really knows how much you struggle, what amount of pain you experience, and how hard it is for you to keep going. You know what your problems have cost you emotionally, physically, psychologically, financially, interpersonally, and spiritually. If you had to rate the severity of pain, difficulty, or loss you've experienced on a scale of 1 to 10, where 1 is minimal and 10 is too much to bear (or "I'd rather be dead"), how would you score your experience? By and large, the higher the number, the more likely it is that you need some chemical intervention, at least for a while.

Lots of us are reluctant to take psychotropic medications. We tell ourselves, as Christina did, that we ought to be able to manage without drugs. We see our need as a weakness, flaw, or laziness. But I know for sure, in the deepest recesses of my being, that no one wants to suffer or do a bad job. If you're overwhelmed with distress or pain, are unable to accomplish your goals, or have trouble participating in what usually matters to you, something is going on that you can't control. You may need medication. Perhaps it's time to work on acceptance of your need and openness to pharmacological management.

You might be concerned about the risks of serious side effects with drug treatment. While you may realize that intervention is necessary, you could also be scared or confused about how to evaluate the dangers. I want to teach you something that I do to minimize risk: I *never* use a *newer* medication to treat a problem when there are *older* available drugs that work *just as well*. Newer is not necessarily better—in fact, it's often worse. The longer a substance has been around, the more people will have taken it. Time gives us the opportunity to identify problems that might not have shown up in the smaller clinical trials or drug tests that are required to get the pill on the market. So if a drug is a necessary piece of your Take-Charge program, choose one that's been around for a while.

I want you to do something else that I do to minimize serious risk with medication: Monitor side effects regularly and frequently with all new prescriptions. Even the reports you may have heard about anti-depressants causing increased suicidal thoughts found that the side effect came on early and escalated in severity over time. In the clinical trials, where there was careful and frequent monitoring of the patients, no one who developed this problem took his or her life. As soon as the thoughts came, the medicine was stopped. The side effect resolved once the medication was discontinued.

In Step 3, you'll find a table that you can use to rate your degree of benefit and the severity of side effects with medication. I urge you to use this monitoring tool as you take charge of your emotional life. Risks can be scary, but you can do a lot to minimize them, and you may need medication. While you need to be cautious, I don't want you to hesitate to treat your difficulties. You deserve to heal!

The assessments you've just completed will help you avoid losing time to illness the way that a woman I recently spoke with did. Last night, Michelle called in to my weekly radio show. She'd just decided to begin medication treatment for bipolar disorder (or manic-depressive illness). She shared that she'd been given the diagnosis a long time beforehand, but hadn't wanted to take drugs. She had "done everything else": She left a job she didn't like, trained for a new career, and pursued lots of self-healing and care.

In spite of it all, she found herself so depressed that she was unable to work or attend exciting job interviews. She realized that she needed to start medication because she "had no choice." I congratulated her on her willingness to take this step. Drugs can do a lot to make manic-depressive illness better.

This disorder is associated with extreme episodes of depression and a high risk of suicide. While Michelle couldn't control her vulnerability to the problem, she was able do a lot to help herself live a full life! I was grateful for her call. She needed the support that I could give, and her story was helpful to many other listeners struggling with a similar dilemma.

Before we move on to look at how you can use medication to treat depression, anxiety, ADD, and nonspecific problems that fall outside of a diagnostic category, I'd like you to pause and recap what you've learned so far in Steps 1 and 2. Complete these sentences and the chart:

1. I've considered my story and its lessons. I've learned:

   _____

   _____

2. I've identified my problems or possible diagnoses. They are:

   _____

   _____

3. I've created my list of target symptoms. It includes:

   _____

   _____

4. I've taken time to rate the severity of my symptoms on a scale of 1 to 10. I'll fill in the chart on the next page to document my experience.

SYMPTOM	TODAY'S SCORE	WORST IT'S EVER BEEN	BEST IT'S EVER BEEN

5. When I begin to evaluate my need for medication and look at the severity of my *overall distress* on a scale of 1 to 10, where 1 is minimal and 10 is unbearable, I score a _____. This means that I may need to be open to my need for medication. **True** or **False** (circle the correct answer)

In the next step, I'll be teaching you how to use medication in your Take-Charge program, since you're probably wondering how it works, how you should take it, and when you should stop it. Let's take a look at that now.

STEP 3

Follow Treatment Guidelines When Medication Is Necessary

In Step 2 of your Take-Charge program, you considered your need for medication. Perhaps you decided that it's a crucial piece of your healing plan, or you think that it might help. In this step, you'll learn some guidelines to follow when taking medicine. They're found in the answers to the following questions:

1. *How do* medicines work for anxiety, depression, and ADD?

2. *How well* do drugs work for these problems?

3. *How much* is enough?

4. What about *side effects?*

5. How do I pick the *right one(s)?*

6. *How long* should I take a medicine?

7. What is involved in *starting and stopping?*

8. Could I need medication even if *I don't have a diagnosis?*

Let's take a look at the answers to these questions. For each one, I've included important guidelines for you to follow if a prescription is part of your Take-Charge program.

HOW DO MEDICATIONS WORK
FOR ANXIETY, DEPRESSION, AND ADD?

The simple answer, and the most truthful one, is that we don't know. We have some pretty good ideas about how different drugs affect brain chemistry and neurotransmitter levels, and we think that some of these actions on nerve cells and chemicals in the brain lead to the benefits or improvement in symptoms that we see. But the human body is extremely complex, and we aren't very sophisticated in deciphering its many secrets.

That said, we do know some important things about how different pharmaceuticals work, and you need to learn some of that information to be your own best advocate! Here's a fundamental fact: *Different classes of medications work differently.* Some have a direct effect on the brain, while others are indirect. This concept explains how quickly a drug can begin to work, and how you'll need to use it.

A medication that has a direct effect binds or attaches itself to a receptor on a nerve cell and causes an immediate change by being there. Substances that work in this way cause a rapid (within minutes to hours) change in symptoms. To understand what I mean, think about alcohol for a moment. Like some other drugs, it has a direct effect on the nerve cells in the brain. So within 30 minutes of drinking some wine or beer, you might feel calmer, giddier, or more relaxed.

Another property of this type of drugs is that once they're metabolized, and thus removed from their receptor spots on the nerves, their benefit disappears and symptoms return. Think about wine or beer again: When you have a couple of drinks, you may feel calm or giddy for a while. But within an hour or two (the length of time depends on your rate of metabolism), you'll be back to your baseline or usual self. To feel different again, you'll need to have another drink or two.

What about drugs that have an indirect effect? These substances work by causing a series of things to happen. They, too, bind to receptors on the nerve cell. But unlike direct-effect medications, their presence begins a cascade of changes that ultimately shifts the neurochemical balance. Think of a superlong row of dominos, falling in *very slow* motion as each piece hits the one next to it. Eventually they all fall down, and the landscape shifts.

Indirect-effect drugs cause all sorts of cellular changes before their ultimate result is seen. They often alter the levels of chemical messengers that are being produced and released into the space between the nerve cells in the brain. These shifts in chemical balance are probably responsible for the improvement in symptoms, but it can take weeks to see this result.

So how does this lesson about direct- and indirect-effect drugs relate to the treatment of depression, anxiety, and ADD? Well, many of the medications used to treat anxiety problems, and almost all of the medications used to treat ADD, are direct-effect drugs. That means they work quickly but don't last long. To achieve a consistent benefit, you have to keep taking them.

By contrast, all the medications used to treat depression—some of which are also used to treat anxiety problems—are indirect drugs. That means they can take days or weeks to bring about a noticeable change, but the benefit isn't short-lived.

This difference in the mechanism of action in various drugs is very important. It explains why the antidepressant you were prescribed last week may not have changed your symptoms yet, whereas the Ativan or Valium you were prescribed to take the edge off your anxiety is working like a dream. This is also the reason why the Ritalin or Adderall prescribed for your ADD, which you take with breakfast each day, works well to improve your focus, concentration, and memory throughout the morning but does nothing for you at the dinner table if you forget your afternoon dose.

So the take-home message in answer to the first question, *How do medicines work?* is that some of them act directly and quickly but don't last that long. Others function indirectly by creating an ongoing shift in neurochemistry and take a while to improve symptoms. Their effect is more lasting.

Important guidelines: Once you've identified the diagnosis or reason that you need medication and have a prescription to address it, be sure you know the answers to these questions:

1. How quickly is the drug meant to work?

2. How often do I need to take it?

3. Do the time frame and mechanism of action fit with my need for relief?

If the answer to the third question is no, please request a different or additional prescription! You may need to take both a direct- and an indirect-effect drug together until the latter starts to work, or even indefinitely to cover a mix of symptoms. Your need depends on your story. Use your knowledge of yourself as you partner with your care provider to create your optimal and unique Take-Charge medication plan.

HOW WELL DO DRUGS WORK FOR ANXIETY, DEPRESSION, AND ADD?

This is a crucial question. Medications can be lifesavers for lots of people, but they aren't magic bullets. Even the best antidepressants, for example, don't work for everyone. Studies comparing them to placebos in individuals with clinical depression show that the real thing works only modestly better than a fake. Not everyone responds to medication, and some individuals respond to sugar pills when they think they're getting a drug!

Furthermore, even when patients respond, all of their symptoms may not go away completely. Often people get *somewhat* better. That said, 18 or 19 million Americans suffer from depression each year. If just 60 percent of them take medication and partially respond to it, that's more than 10 million who have changed for the better. And depression is one of the greatest causes of morbidity and mortality in the world, so a lot of lives would be transformed or saved. In fact, a huge study of 65,000 individuals that was published in *The American Journal of Psychiatry* in January 2006 found that treatment with antidepressant drugs did reduce the risk of suicide in depressed teenagers and adults. Just remember that this treatment option *can* be a lifesaver, but it's not a miracle cure. It's simply a piece of the puzzle.

The same goes for anxiety disorders: Medication is a godsend for many folks and somewhat helpful for others. Most sufferers get some benefit from short-acting medicines, but these are bad choices if your condition is ongoing and long lasting. You'll get rebound anxiety, or an increase in those feelings, when the drug wears off.

Many anxious people do well on what we call antidepressants. These are good choices for chronic, ongoing anxiety. In fact, there's really no good reason for the drugs to be linked only to depression. Although most were first created to treat mood problems, studies have shown them to help a lot of other troubles, too. For example, they're beneficial for obsessive-compulsive disorder (an anxiety condition), panic disorder, and social phobia.

What about medication for ADD? Well, again, popping a pill isn't the whole answer. The vast majority (over 90 percent) of sufferers will get *some* benefit from stimulants such as Ritalin and Dexedrine; occasionally other types of medication are helpful, too. While drugs don't eliminate all the symptoms, most patients can focus better and control their impulsivity more easily when they take something.

How does medication do in treating manic-depressive illness? Although bipolar disorder involves periods of depression, it's different from what we call unipolar depression. Because it's cyclical in nature, we often need to use several substances together and adjust them over time to treat this illness. While drugs don't prevent depression or mania, they surely decrease the severity and frequency of symptoms. Remember, this illness has a high risk for suicide. Many people suffering from it need to take a mood stabilizer such as lithium in addition to their antidepressant. While medicine isn't the whole story, it's usually critical.

So the take-home message in the answer to the second question: *How well do drugs work?* is "Pretty well." Medication can make a huge difference in the symptomatic relief of the mood and anxiety disorders and ADD. It can also decrease the frequency of episodes of mania and depression, although it isn't a panacea. Using this treatment option may make a huge or moderate difference in your life.

Important guidelines: Once you've identified your target symptoms, evaluate each drug and dose you try with the rating scale entitled "My Progress Including Drug, Dose, and Side Effects" that you'll find later in this chapter. If you don't see adequate improvement *on your rating scale* with the proper dose of medication over the appropriate period of time, you may need to try something else or to add another treatment to your plan. Talk to your care provider about your observations and experiences as you use your rating scale to take charge of your emotional life.

HOW MUCH MEDICATION IS ENOUGH?

This may seem like a silly answer, but the right dose is however much you need to feel better. By and large, your level of response will be dose dependent. In other words, the more you take, the greater the benefit you'll experience. But since all medicines have side effects and these are dose dependent, too, you don't want to overshoot your need. If you take more than necessary and feel too ill from side effects, you may not be able to continue using that medication. So you want to "start low and go slow." You'll progressively move the amount up until you see enough improvement without too much fallout.

Although there are recommended starting levels for all medications, these are only useful to a point. Each person has a unique sensitivity to each drug's benefits and set of side effects. Your profile is based on your genetics, biology, and metabolic processes, and there's a great deal of difference from one person to the next. There's no way to predict your response in advance, so finding your right dose will involve trial and error.

Years ago I was treating two tiny, depressed 95-pound women (who didn't know each other) at the same time. Both were taking Prozac when it was only available in a 20-mg capsule. One woman needed four pills or 80 mg a day to treat her depression, and she had no side effects. The other patient had dramatic side effects on a 20-mg dose, but actually needed only 2 mg a day to treat her illness. How could she get such a tiny amount? She'd open the capsule and dump out the granules. Then she'd lick her finger, dip it into the grains, and lick her finger again. She tolerated that amount well and felt she was back to being herself after several weeks.

So how much medication is enough? It all depends on your story. Think of my two tiny ladies: They were the same size, had the same diagnosis, and were taking the same medicine. But one needed 40 times as much Prozac as the other did for healing. It's all about your unique story and body chemistry.

Important guidelines: Once you've begun a medication trial, keep track of your dosage level as you evaluate your improvement in target symptoms. Use the expanded rating scale following the next question to evaluate your improvement and your level of side effects. As you work the Take-Charge program, share your rating scale with your treatment provider. This will help you and your doctor find your best drug and dose.

WHAT ABOUT SIDE EFFECTS?

Every single drug has side effects, but what does that really mean? Remember that each medication is designed to hit a target or decrease certain "target symptoms." But we haven't gotten sophisticated enough in our drug development to create agents that only affect the cells and symptoms we want to change. Therefore, whenever you take a pill—even an aspirin or Tylenol—it will travel throughout your body and touch billions of cells and many metabolic processes. It can cause many upsets as a result of its actions all over the body, and these unintended disturbances are what we call side effects.

If you look at any print advertisement for a drug or open the *Physicians' Desk Reference (PDR)* and look up any medicine, you'll see hundreds of possible side effects, risks, and cautions listed. In current times, this downside is inevitable, because we haven't gotten sophisticated enough to avoid it.

All medications have a bunch of common side effects and a myriad of not-so-common ones. Before you start taking anything, ask your doctor to review the former. Be sure you're comfortable with what you hear before starting the pill, and then keep track of your responses, both positive and negative. You may develop a common side effect, a rare one, or one that's never even been reported. Most of these tend to decrease in severity over time, so if you can tolerate them early on, try to hang in there with your plan. The problems will probably become less prominent.

So the answer to the question: *What about side effects?* is that they're unavoidable and sometimes problematic.

Important guidelines: Use the following rating scale to evaluate your symptom response and side-effect profile with various medication doses. Make as many copies of the chart as you need to document your ongoing experience. Use it to partner with your treatment provider in finding your best course of action as you take charge of your emotional life.

MY PROGRESS: INCLUDING DRUG, DOSE, AND SIDE-EFFECTS RATING SCALE

Use a scale from 1 to 10, where **1 = Almost Never** and **10 = Always,** for target symptoms. List the side effects you experience in each week, and rate them on a scale of 1 to 10, where **1 = Very Mild** and **10 = Intolerable.**

	Date: / /	Date: / /	Date: / /	Date: / /	Date: / /
	Drug & dose	Drug & dose	Drug & dose	Drug & dose	Drug & dose
TARGET SYMPTOMS	Rating	Rating	Rating	Rating	Rating
1.					
2.					
3.					
4.					
5.					
SIDE EFFECTS	Rating	Rating	Rating	Rating	Rating
1.					
2.					
3.					
4.					
5.					

HOW DO I PICK THE RIGHT MEDICINE(S)?

Unfortunately, the answer to this question is similar to the others. Although we doctors have some idea of what to try, we aren't very advanced in this area.

Of course, whatever medication we choose must be one that's effective for your diagnosis. But there will probably be several drugs like that, so what guidelines do we use? Well, first and foremost is your past history. If you formerly responded well to something, there's a good chance that you'll respond to that agent again. By contrast, if you didn't respond positively to a particular medicine before, it's unlikely that you will now.

If your personal past doesn't help, family history sometimes does. You may do well on a drug that's helped a biological relative with similar problems, or do poorly on one that someone you're related to couldn't tolerate.

Many researchers and clinicians are trying to find ways to match symptoms to the best treatment option. Some of their techniques may ultimately be highly effective. But for now, the answer to the question: *How do I pick the right medicine?* is largely diagnosis, history, and hunch.

Important guidelines: Get as much historical data as you can to partner effectively with your doctor, and then vigorously evaluate your progress and problems with every intervention. You can take charge of finding your best fit here, and it's crucial that you do so.

HOW LONG SHOULD I TAKE A MEDICINE?

The duration of a prescription depends on the type, length, and severity of the problem you're being treated for. If you have a chronic or recurrent problem, it may make sense for you to remain on medication indefinitely. This is often the case for people with anxiety disorders, depression, bipolar disorder, and ADD. On the other hand, if you're experiencing a first-time episode of crippling anxiety and depression, then a six-month to one-year course may be appropriate for you.

In another scenario, if you've been prescribed medicine for a brief increase in some ongoing symptoms that are usually tolerable, it might make sense for you to take the drug for an even shorter time. That said, antidepressant medications are rarely meant to be used for less than six months. Remember that they're indirect-effect drugs. They take a while to work, and therefore they only make sense for challenges that are somewhat ongoing.

So the answer to the question: *How long should I take a medicine?* depends on the diagnosis, length, and severity of your problem.

Important guidelines: Be sure that your story and experience of trouble jibes with your treatment provider's recommendations. Your history dictates the type and length of interventions in your Take-Charge program.

WHAT'S INVOLVED IN STARTING AND STOPPING A MEDICATION?

Well, we've covered beginning treatment (start low, go slow) but not the stopping part. This is when you need to know about withdrawal syndromes and reemergence of symptoms.

Medicines that you take episodically (or as needed) for anxiety or sleep can usually be stopped without tapering off. This applies to pills that you don't take every few hours or every day. Similarly, stimulants for ADD can almost always be cut off at any point.

Most drugs that are regular and ongoing, however, shouldn't be stopped abruptly. You might have a withdrawal syndrome or a return of your symptoms if you don't go off slowly. *If it's time for you to try stopping a medication, work with your prescribing doctor to do so at an appropriate rate.* You may discover that you need the drug more than you realized, or that you have to cut your dose much more slowly than you had anticipated.

So the answer to the question, *What's involved in starting and stopping a medicine?* is that it depends on what drug you're taking, and what problem you're trying to treat. There's no one-size-fits-all solution to this process, but there is a perfectly right answer for you.

Important guideline: Include your doctor, and make sure your plan to stop medication fits your story and experience with the drug.

COULD I NEED MEDICATION EVEN IF I DON'T HAVE A DIAGNOSIS?

The answer is a qualified yes. Remember my story: I occasionally take a tiny dose of Valium when my system is too revved up to settle down and sleep. I don't meet diagnostic criteria for an anxiety disorder or anything else, but I do benefit from a pinch of periodic intervention. That could be the case for you, too. However, the answer to this question is a *qualified* yes, because before treating your symptom, you need to rule out a medical or psychiatric condition as its cause. Don't assume that you don't have one. Even when no diagnosis fits, you'll need to identify a specific set of target symptoms to guide your medication use. And of course, you must always evaluate your risk, benefit, and response.

Important guidelines: Make sure you know what symptoms you're treating with the drug. Monitor your need and response just as you would in treating a formal disorder. Just keep in mind that even if you lack a diagnosis, medication might still be a crucial piece of your Take-Charge program.

❧

Congratulations! You've just completed Steps 1, 2, and 3, an intensive course in evaluating your need for medication and learning guidelines for its use. Although you aren't ready to be your own treatment provider, you're highly qualified to partner with your doctor in taking charge of your emotional life.

You've learned how to use four principles to assess your medication requirement. You now know how to include diagnoses, target symptoms, and risk-benefit concerns in finding the right path. You even understand a lot about how medicines work, how much is enough, how to start and stop drugs, and when it makes sense to include pharmacological interventions even if you don't have a diagnosis.

Before moving on to Step 4, please take a moment to respond to the statements on the next page either on the lines provided or on a separate piece of paper.

1. When I evaluated my need for medication with the four principles, I realized that:

    _____

    _____

    _____

2. When I review the eight questions and answers in Step 3, my take-home lessons and guidelines are:

    _____

    _____

    _____

You've just taken stock of where you are with diagnostic and pharmacological issues. Without further ado, let's move into Step 4 and see what you can add to your Take-Charge plan!

STEP 4

Include Complementary- and Alternative-Medicine Interventions

Welcome to Step 4 of your Take-Charge program, where you'll learn all about complementary and alternative medicine (CAM). Before I teach you what CAM is, why it matters, and how to use it, I need to give you some background. I want you to understand how these options came to be separated from mainstream medicine in the United States.

You see, our current health-care system, with its focus on disease, illness, and chemical intervention, is relatively new. Until the 19th century, natural, folk, and home remedies played a significant role in achieving and maintaining wellness. Herbs, plants, dietary restrictions, spiritual practices, and intuitive interventions were intrinsic to this model. Over the years, through trial and error, what worked became accepted practice. Lessons were passed from generation to generation, and healers carried that acquired wisdom forward. The care provider was felt to support the individual's innate capacity to recover. As far back as 400 B.C., Hippocrates said that the "natural forces within us are the true healers of disease." Hippocrates, Aristotle, and Galen (a classical Greek physician and writer) were all holistic. They saw the body, mind, and spirit as interrelated—or maybe even as one!

In the mid-1600s, the philosopher René Descartes began a movement to separate the soul-mind (which became the responsibility of the church or religion) and the body (which became the concern of science) from one another. He espoused an approach that viewed human bodies as resembling clocks. When a clock broke, you were to take out the broken piece and replace it. Then voilà—it was fixed! When a person became ill, you were to excise, replace, or treat the sick *piece,* and the patient would be healed. This reductionist view took hold fast.

As science began to advance, medical and surgical interventions became the cornerstones of Western medicine; natural, holistic, and folk practices began to take a backseat. Since many of those approaches had evolved by trial and error over countless generations, as opposed to being created by technological design, they were often discounted by scientists and the medical establishment. Their value hadn't been rigorously proven, so they couldn't possibly be of merit.

In spite of this devaluation, many native healers and practitioners of CAM persisted in their work, and a variety of new CAM providers began to emerge. But most schools of Western medicine ignored this growing movement. The lessons of these other approaches were left out of the routine training of doctors. As a result, mainstream physicians didn't learn how to deal with these other disciplines.

The growing divide between enduring, ancient wisdom and modern-day allopathic medicine gave birth to the confusion and discontent that many of us feel today. Eventually, this split led to the CAM movement. Lots of folks within the medical community and outside of it who saw value in the disregarded interventions began to demand attention, consideration, and study. As a result, the National Institutes of Health established the National Center for Complementary and Alternative Medicine (NCCAM). This center was created to explore complementary and alternative healing practices in the context of rigorous science, train CAM researchers, and disseminate authoritative information to the public and professionals.

The NCCAM has defined CAM and organized it into five major modalities. The following information comes from one of the center's publications, titled: "Get the Facts: What is Complementary and Alternative Medicine?" You can find the full text at **www.NCCAM.nih.gov/health/whatiscam**. I've added the *italicized* information to the text; you'll find definitions of many of the terms in the Glossary at the end of this book.

WHAT IS COMPLEMENTARY AND ALTERNATIVE MEDICINE?

Complementary and alternative medicine, as defined by NCCAM, is a group of diverse medical and health-care systems, practices, and products that aren't presently considered to be part of conventional medicine. While some scientific evidence exists regarding some CAM therapies, for most there are key questions that are yet to be answered through well-designed scientific studies—questions such as whether these therapies are safe and whether they work for the diseases or medical conditions for which they're used.

The list of what's considered to be CAM changes continually, as those therapies that are proven to be safe and effective are adopted into conventional health care and as new approaches emerge.

IS COMPLEMENTARY MEDICINE DIFFERENT FROM ALTERNATIVE MEDICINE?

Yes, the two are different.

- **Complementary** medicine is used **together with** conventional medicine. An example of complementary therapy is using aromatherapy to help lessen a patient's discomfort following surgery. *Other examples include using yoga with an antidepressant to treat depressive illness, adding regular singing to medication interventions for panic disorder, and cutting down on sweets while taking medication to decrease the symptoms of ADD.*

- **Alternative** medicine is used **in place of** conventional medicine. An example of alternative therapy is using a special diet to treat cancer instead of undergoing surgery, radiation, or chemotherapy that has been recommended by a conventional doctor. *Other examples include using SAM-e (a dietary supplement) to treat ADD and exercise to treat moderate depression.*

WHAT IS INTEGRATIVE MEDICINE?

Integrative medicine, as defined by NCCAM, combines mainstream medical therapies and CAM therapies for which there's some high-quality scientific evidence of safety and effectiveness. *This is what I do in my clinical practice, and what you're doing as you use the ten-step approach to create your personal Take-Charge program.*

WHAT ARE THE MAJOR TYPES OF COMPLEMENTARY AND ALTERNATIVE MEDICINE?

NCCAM classifies CAM therapies into five categories, or domains:

1. Alternative medical systems. These are built upon complete systems of theory and practice. Often, these systems have evolved apart from and earlier than the conventional-medical approach used in the United States. Examples of alternative medical systems that have developed in Western cultures include homeopathic and naturopathic medicine. Examples of systems that have developed in non-Western cultures include traditional Chinese medicine and Ayurveda.

2. Mind-body interventions. Mind-body medicine uses a variety of techniques designed to enhance the mind's capacity to affect bodily function and symptoms. Some techniques that were considered CAM in the past have become mainstream (for example, patient-support groups and cognitive-behavioral therapy). Other mind-body techniques are still considered CAM, including meditation; prayer; mental healing; and therapies that use creative outlets such as art, music, or dance.

3. Biologically based therapies. These use substances found in nature, such as herbs, foods, and vitamins. Some examples include dietary supplements, herbal products, and the use of other so-called natural but as yet scientifically unproven therapies (for example, using shark cartilage to treat cancer). *Other examples include using SAM-e, vitamin B_{12}, folate, and omega-3 fatty acids in the treatment of depression; using Chinese herbs to regulate hormonal imbalances that affect mood; and decreasing carbohydrate consumption while increasing protein intake to regulate both mood and attentional symptoms.*

4. Manipulative and body-based methods. These are based on physical manipulation and/or movement of one or more parts of the body. Some examples include chiropractic or osteopathic manipulation and massage.

5. Energy therapies. These involve the use of energy fields. They're of two types:

— **Biofield therapies** are intended to affect energy fields that purportedly surround and penetrate the human body. The existence of such fields hasn't yet been scientifically proven. Some forms of energy therapy manipulate biofields by applying pressure and/or moving the body by placing the hands in, or through, these fields. Examples include qi gong, Reiki, and therapeutic touch.

— **Bioelectromagnetic-based therapies** involve the unconventional use of electromagnetic fields, such as pulsed fields, magnetic fields, or alternating-current or direct-current fields.

SOURCES OF NCCAM INFORMATION

NCCAM Clearinghouse
Toll-free in the U.S.: 1-888-644-6226
International: 301-519-3153

TTY (for hearing-impaired callers): 1-866-464-3615
E-mail: **info@nccam.nih.gov**
Website: **nccam.nih.gov**
Address: NCCAM Clearinghouse, P.O. Box 7923, Gaithersburg, MD,
   20898-7923
Fax: 1-866-464-3616
Fax-on-Demand service: 1-888-644-6226

The clearinghouse provides information on CAM and on NCCAM. Services include fact sheets, other publications, and the ability to search federal databases of scientific and medical literature. It doesn't provide medical advice, treatment recommendations, or referrals to practitioners.

Congratulations! You now know more about CAM than most people. Before moving on, use the following space (or a separate piece of paper) to record your CAM experiences, listing all the interventions you've used to date. Which ones have worked or caused you problems? Do any still serve you well?

_____

_____

_____

_____

_____

Now think about how CAM came to be split off from current-day Western medical practice. Does this division between modalities disturb you as much as it does me? When I was a medical student at the University of Pennsylvania, I was so troubled by the limitations of the model I was learning that I took outside courses in massage therapy and Chinese medicine. I needed to balance the Western approach with one that focused on the whole person; the intrinsic capacity to heal; the wonder of wellness; and the power of faith, energy, and touch to make a difference. I always try to combine the lessons of ancient wisdom with the science of modern medicine, because I believe all disciplines contain offerings that can enhance our lives and our work. Do you agree?

Before examining the specific modalities that will be the focus of Step 4, let's look at the frequency of CAM use in the United States. As you consider the statistics, you may be struck by the number of people who actively include these options in their lives. Many of us are looking for more integration! The most used intervention is prayer, and since spirituality and prayer are so crucial to healing, I've devoted a whole chapter to them. This will be your focus in Step 10.

The information on the next page comes from a report titled "The Use of Complementary and Alternative Medicine in the United States" (reviewed July 2004, updated September 2004). The survey was completed by 31,044 adults in the U.S. The full text can be found at **www. nccam.nih.gov**. (I added the italicized comments.)

Respondents answered questions on various types of CAM therapies commonly used in the United States. These included provider-based therapies, such as acupuncture and chiropractic, and other therapies that don't require a provider, such as natural products, special diets, and megavitamin therapy. The number of interventions included was quite significant. How many of them are familiar to you?

∽

CAM THERAPIES INCLUDED IN THE 2002 NATIONAL HEALTH INTERVIEW SURVEY (NHIS)
AN ASTERISK (*) INDICATES A PRACTITIONER-BASED THERAPY.

Acupuncture*	Massage*
Ayurveda*	Meditation
Biofeedback*	Megavitamin therapy
Chelation therapy*	Natural products
Chiropractic care*	(nonvitamin and nonmineral, such
Deep-breathing exercises	as herbs and other products from
Diet-based therapies	plants, enzymes, etc.)
Vegetarian diet	Naturopathy*
Macrobiotic diet	Prayer for health reasons
Atkins diet	Prayed for own health
Pritikin diet	Others ever prayed for your health
Ornish diet	Participate in prayer group
Zone diet	Healing ritual for self
Energy healing therapy*	Progressive relaxation
Folk medicine*	Qi gong
Guided imagery	Reiki*
Homeopathic treatment	Tai chi
Hypnosis*	Yoga

— **How many people use CAM.** In the United States, 36% of adults are using some form of CAM. When megavitamin therapy and prayer specifically for health reasons are included, that number rises to 62%.

While the NHIS did not include questions on spending, a 1997 survey found that the American public spent $36 billion to $47 billion on CAM, and these numbers have continued to rise. Of this amount, between $12 billion and $20 billion was paid out of pocket for the services of professional CAM health-care providers. This is more money than people paid from their own funds for all hospitalizations in 1997, and about half the amount of all noncovered physician services. Five billion dollars of out-of-pocket spending was on herbal products.

— **CAM domains used the most.** When prayer is included in the definition of CAM, the domain of mind-body medicine is the most commonly used (53%). Excluding prayer, biologically based therapies (22%) are more popular than mind-body medicine (17%).

— **CAM therapies used the most.** Prayer specifically for health reasons was the most common. The majority of people who use these therapies do so to treat themselves, as only about 12% of the survey respondents sought care from a licensed CAM practitioner. The ten most common choices were:

1. Prayer for oneself: 43.0%
2. Prayer for oneself by others: 24.4%
3. Natural products: 18.9%
4. Deep-breathing exercises: 11.6%
5. Prayer in groups for oneself : 9.6%
6. Meditation: 7.6%
7. Chiropractic care: 7.5%
8. Yoga: 5.1%
9. Massage: 5%
10. Diet-based therapies: 3.5%

— **Health conditions prompting CAM use.** In the U.S., people are most likely to use these methods for back, neck, head, or joint aches, or other painful conditions; colds; anxiety or depression; gastrointestinal disorders; or sleeping problems.

— **Reasons for using CAM.** When people were asked to select from five reasons to describe why they used CAM, results were as follows (respondents could select more than one reason):

•   55 percent felt that it would improve health when used in combination with conventional medical treatments.

•   50 percent said it would be interesting to try.

The survey found that most people use CAM along with conventional medicine rather than in place of it.

INTEGRATING CAM INTO YOUR TAKE-CHARGE PROGRAM

Now that you know what CAM is and how widely it's used, you're ready to dive into examining its place in your Take-Charge program. Like most people, you probably believe that combining CAM with conventional medicine can help you—I sure do. So how should you include these interventions in your life?

The reach and depth of CAM is huge. We can't possibly cover all the domains and specific modalities in just one chapter. Since there are many entire texts devoted to alternative medical systems such as Chinese medicine (for example, *Between Heaven and Earth,* by Harriet Beinfield and Efrem Korngold) and Ayurveda (as in Deepak Chopra's work), we won't focus on that domain except to look at yoga. Keep in mind that alternative medical systems have a great deal to offer. You might find through your own research that one of these approaches speaks to you and offers interventions that work. I encourage you to explore what calls out to you.

Similarly, we won't be studying the energy therapies, but for a different reason. These approaches are among the most controversial of CAM practices because we haven't yet been able to demonstrate the presence or effect of energy fields. Remember, however, that this lack of "proof" doesn't tell us anything about the value of the domain. Energy healing has been a part of almost all societies and religions for thousands of years. For example, Chinese medicine is organized around the life-force energy it calls *chi* (pronounced "chee"). Asian Indians focus on *prana,* and the Judeo-Christian traditions value the energy described as halos around powerful people.

In spite of the controversy, these methods are growing in popularity and are actively being studied in medical centers around the country. The 2002 survey found that 4.6 percent of participants had used some form of healing ritual, 1 percent had used Reiki, and 0.5 percent had used qi gong. In the integrative medicine program at the University of Arizona School of Medicine where I teach, my Chinese medicine colleagues often recommend qi gong to our clinic patients. So if one of the energy interventions appeals to you, I encourage you to explore it; perhaps you'll find some healing there.

In the rest of this chapter you'll consider the role that some specific CAM interventions could play in your Take-Charge program. The modalities you'll examine are:

- Music

- Yoga

- Biologically based therapies: Saint-John's-wort, SAM-e, vitamins, omega-3 fatty acids, and nutritional interventions

- Exercise

- Guided imagery, meditation, and other relaxation techniques

- Massage

- Light therapy

I've chosen these representative CAM interventions because they're reasonably well understood and easy to implement. The list isn't meant to be exhaustive, but rather to expose you to some options, so don't allow yourself to be confined by the limits of this particular selection. Consider each intervention, but as you do so, keep thinking about how to create the best and broadest Take-Charge plan for your needs. (As I mentioned earlier, you'll examine prayer and spiritual practices in Step 10.)

MUSIC

Music plays a crucial role in every culture and in most spiritual traditions. It's deeply healing. In fact, chanting and drumming have been among the major tools of practitioners such as shamans for thousands of years. Recent studies have shown that music affects immune function, pain thresholds, cognitive function, blood pressure, and levels of anxiety and depression. In *Molecules of Emotion,* Candace Pert describes how music and meditation bring about their healing benefits. These practices actually activate the natural feel-good chemicals in the brain, called "endorphins"!

There are many ways for you to include this modality in your Take-Charge plan. You can turn on your CD player or radio and listen to calming pieces to help you settle your nervous system. Choose energetic and lively ones when you're feeling down or blue and need a boost, and turn on background music for better focus. This last technique helps many ADD sufferers concentrate better.

You can also create the sounds yourself by playing an instrument or singing. While all forms of music can be healing, playing a wind instrument or using your voice is especially helpful if you're hoping to calm an agitated state. These activities force you to breathe slowly and deeply and to relax your chest muscles. This process settles your nervous system in the same way that breathing into a paper bag interrupts a panic attack.

You can even whistle! In the musical *The King and I,* the heroine, Anna, whistles a happy tune whenever she feels afraid. In trying to fool those around her by presenting a calm and in-control demeanor, she settles her nervous system so much that her fear actually disappears.

When I do workshops, I often have the group sing with me. In this way, we step out of the thinking mode and into the doing-being mode together. As a beautiful melody fills the room, participants often rediscover how crucial music has been to their wellness. The exercise teaches them to include this art form in their Take-Charge plans.

I sing in a choir. No matter how lousy I feel when I head to practice, I always feel better on the way home. This recurring experience has taught me how much I need to sing for my mental well-being.

There's actually a whole field of music therapy. Practice guidelines have been established by the American Music Therapy Association (AMTA). You can find more information here:

- American Music Therapy Association: **www.musictherapy.org**

- The International Arts-Medicine Association: **www.members.aol.com/iamaorg**

- The Society for the Arts in Healthcare: **www.thesah.org**

Each of us is unique, so we each heal differently. Consider how music might fit into *your* Take-Charge plan. Think about what kind of tunes you like and how you feel when you hear, play, or sing them. What about the sound gives you pleasure? Write your reflections below.

_____

_____

_____

_____

Perhaps you realize that music should be included in your plan, and you may have committed to a regular practice. If so, bravo! If not, don't worry; it may not be your thing.

Let's move on to consider the role of yoga in healing.

YOGA

Yoga practice is on the upswing in the Western world today. Teachers, practices, and options abound for including it in your life. You can find classes in studios, retreat centers, online, and at your local gym; aspects of this discipline have even been combined with aerobic exercise in some popular courses.

But what *is* yoga, and how might you want to use it in your Take-Charge plan? Well, it was developed and has been practiced in India for thousands of years. The name means "union with the divine," and it's based on the philosophy that we create our experiences by the decisions we make in life. It sees the self as a "seed," or piece of the divine with infinite potential, and encourages personal development as the path to peace and self-actualization. The philosophy focuses on acceptance, self-observation without judgment, compassion, connecting with oneness, and deep centering.

This ancient system uses breathing exercises, posture, stretches, and meditation to balance the body's energy centers. There are many forms of practice, and you may find that a particular one appeals to you. Yoga has been used in combination with other treatments for depression, anxiety, and stress for years.

SUDARSHAN KRIYA

A particular type of yogic breathing called Sudarshan Kriya (SKY) has been studied and shown to relieve depression, anxiety, stress, and post-traumatic stress disorder (PTSD). While it's a very powerful healing technique, it can also exacerbate mania. Please don't use it if you are a rapid cycler or have bipolar disorder. It can also lead to a drop in blood levels of lithium, so if you're taking this medication, you shouldn't use it either. If you're bipolar but stable on medications other than lithium, yogic breathing might be an option for you, but please check with your doctor to be sure it's safe for you to experiment before attempting to use this tool.

So what is yogic breathing anyway? SKY consists of a specific sequence and order of breathing patterns designed to calm the nervous system, promote attention, and increase the sensation of pleasure. I first learned about SKY at a course I attended at the annual meeting of the American Psychiatric Association in May 2004. Richard Brown, M.D., and Patricia Gerbarg, M.D., who have written extensively about SKY, taught the course. (See "Complementary and Alternative Treatments in Psychiatry" that Brown, Gerbarg, and Muskin wrote for the book *Psychiatry,* 2nd edition.)

If you're interested, you can learn how to practice SKY through the Art of Living Foundation. This nonprofit organization is affiliated with the United Nations and teaches SKY techniques in over 100 countries. In fact, volunteers offered free courses to hundreds of traumatized and grieving New Yorkers after the terrorist attacks of September 11, 2001. For course information, visit **www.artofliving.org**. You may even discover a yoga instructor in your community who can teach you this technique.

EVALUATING YOGA

You'll find many books, CDs, and other resources to help you decide whether to include yoga of some kind in your Take-Charge plan. But, before you buy a lot of materials, I suggest that you check out a few classes. See if the practice appeals to you. It may, or it may not. For example, while I deeply resonate with music, I don't with yoga. I've tried a number of classes over the years, and although I enjoyed them,

I haven't felt drawn in enough to begin a regular practice. But my story may not be yours, so check it out and see. Lots of people love it!

At this point, pause and consider whether to include yoga in *your* Take-Charge plan. Think about your experiences, if any, with the practice. Do you enjoy it? Do you wish to learn more about its potential benefits? Might you want to find a class, teacher, or retreat? Use the space below (or a separate piece of paper) to record your thoughts.

_____

_____

_____

_____

Perhaps you realize that yoga belongs in your Take-Charge plan, or maybe you want to learn more about it. If so, terrific! If not, that's fine too; it may not be your thing.

Let's move on to consider the role of nutritional and biologically based therapies, including SAM-e, Saint-John's-wort, vitamins, and omega-3 fatty acids.

NUTRITIONAL ADJUSTMENTS

We're obsessed with food, diets, and the ideal way to eat for optimal health and weight loss. There are countless books on this subject, and the diet industry thrives in our culture.

While we can't possibly cover all that's known about nutrition and mental well-being, let's review a couple of crucial points. First, anxiety and ADD are made worse by excessive caffeine consumption, and depression is often exacerbated by alcohol intake. Please examine your use of these substances in relation to your struggles.

Second, ADD, mood, and anxiety symptoms are exacerbated when our diets are loaded with carbohydrates and deficient in protein. For detailed guidance on how to adjust your diet for optimal health, I recommend Christiane Northrup's book *The Wisdom of Menopause*, and Daniel Amen's books *Healing ADD* and *Healing Anxiety and Depression* (with Lisa Routh). Dr. Northrup, for example, recommends a diet composed of 40% protein, 35% low-glycemic-index carbs, and 25% fat for optimal mood balance in women during the perimenopausal and menopausal years. I've had great results following this regimen.

I recommend that you begin to keep track of the relationship between your food choices and your symptoms. Some minor adjustments in your meal and snack choices can make a major difference to your well-being.

BIOLOGICALLY BASED THERAPIES

I've chosen to include some biologically based therapies in your Step 4 exploration because there's growing interest in using nutritional and dietary supplements for wellness. In fact, U.S. sales of these products in 2002 were $18.7 billion, with herbal/botanical supplements accounting for $4.3 billion. We're anxious to take substances that we think of as natural, healing, and less dangerous than prescription medications. But we need to be aware of what we assume will work, and the risks we may tend to minimize. That said, several nutritional adjustments and supplements have been shown to make a difference in mental well-being.

SAINT-JOHN'S-WORT

This herb (*Hypericum performatum* in Latin) has been used for centuries for medicinal purposes, including the treatment of depression. (See the NCCAM for the fact sheet on Saint-John's-wort that's excerpted here.)

Here are some key points about it:

- The composition of Saint-John's-wort and how it might work aren't well understood.

- There is some scientific evidence that the herb is useful for treating mild to moderate depression. However, recent studies suggest that it's of no benefit in treating major depression of moderate severity. More research is required to help us know whether it has value in treating other forms of depression.

- Saint-John's-wort interacts with certain drugs, and these interactions can be dangerous.

- It's important to inform all your health-care providers about any therapy that you're currently using or considering, including any dietary supplements. This is to help ensure a safe and coordinated course of care.

If you'd like to try Saint-John's-wort, please be sure to discuss it with your doctor. This herb can interfere with some heart and cancer medications, decrease the effectiveness of birth-control pills, and be occasionally toxic when used together with some prescription anti-depressants. That said, it's been used successfully in Europe for many years and could be a good choice for you.

SAM-e

SAM-e was discovered in 1952 and has been widely used in Europe for the treatment of depression, arthritis, and liver disease. It's an essential molecule in all living cells in the human body. We get about one-third of the amount our bodies need from our diets, and our livers produce a lot as well. But some people may be deficient in SAM-e and need supplementation; you could be one of them. This substance was approved by the FDA as a nutraceutical in 1998. You can purchase it over the counter without a prescription.

SAM-e has been shown to be an effective antidepressant by itself. In fact, some people respond to it who haven't done well with prescription medication. It's also been found to be useful in increasing some patients' responses to prescription antidepressants when taken in combination with them. I occasionally add SAM-e to such a drug when I've gotten a partial response and can't go up on the medication dose.

This supplement should always be taken with B_{12} and folate, since these vitamins are necessary for it to be effective. These can also be bought over the counter.

SAM-e is less dangerous than Saint-John's-wort in terms of drug interactions, but it shouldn't be used by bipolar individuals because it can cause mania. For more information, visit:

- NCCAM Clearinghouse: **www.nccam.nih.gov**
- CAM on PubMed: **www.nlm.nih.gov/nccam/camon pubmed.html**
- Office of Dietary Supplements (ODS), National Institutes of Health (NIH): **www.ods.od.nih.gov**

B₁₂ AND FOLATE

You may be taking these vitamins already, but it's worth knowing that they can help your mood substantially. Folate brightens your outlook when used alone, can improve antidepressant response, and may increase your response to SAM-e. The usual dose is 800 mcg to 5 mg a day.

Vitamin B_{12} can improve mood and enhance energy when used alone. It may also increase the antidepressant response of SAM-e.

If you're struggling with mood issues, you might want to try adding these two supplements to your Take-Charge program. They're well tolerated and can make a big difference.

OMEGA-3 FATTY ACIDS

We're hearing a lot of talk about the health benefits of omega-3 fatty acids or fish oil found in cold-water fish such as salmon and tuna. Supplementation is effective in treating depression in people whose diets are deficient in this oil, but we don't know whether taking a pill is enough by itself. Antidepressants may also be necessary.

I sometimes encourage people on antidepressants to add fish oil to their Take-Charge programs to get a further boost in mood. A 1,000 mg capsule containing the two fatty acids eicosapentaenoic acid (EPA) and docosahexaenoic acid (DHA) is a good dose. Be careful not to take more than 2,000 mg a day from supplements in order to avoid problems with excess bleeding.

For a free software download that contains information about the omega-3 fatty acid content of foods visit: **http://efaeducation.nih. gov/sig/kim.html**.

❧

Having looked at a smattering of biologically based therapies, I'd like you to pause and consider what role these agents might play in *your* Take-Charge plan. Write your thoughts below, or on a separate piece of paper.

_____

_____

_____

_____

Perhaps you've decided to include or abandon the use of an herb or supplement, or maybe you have no interest in including biological interventions at all. Whatever feels right for you is fine.

EXERCISE

We all know that exercise is good for our general health. It helps with weight control, blood-pressure reduction, and keeping our hearts healthy. You may also recognize that regular movement improves your mood, reduces your stress level, and helps you focus. The importance of physical activity for a sound body, mind, and spirit has been recognized for countless generations, and was a cornerstone of ancient Greek culture. Their wisdom has been passed forward and continues to be manifest in the universal appeal of the Olympic Games.

I've been personally aided at times of great stress and depression by intense aerobic exercise of 30 minutes' duration, five days a week. My patients have routinely and consistently had similar experiences. Additionally, ADD sufferers I've treated experience improvement in their ability to focus and control their impulses on their regular workout days.

Recently, a series of studies has even shown that exercise has an "antidepressant" effect. In other words, regular intensive aerobic activity has been found to reduce the symptoms of *moderate* depression, *just as well as antidepressant medication,* in some people. Of course, many depressed individuals can't motivate themselves enough to exercise regularly, and some who can may still need to employ additional tools and interventions. But the take-home message is that whether you use medicine or not, routine physical activity can make a huge difference to your mental well-being.

What role might exercise play in your Take-Charge program? Think about your experiences getting your body moving. Have you played sports, walked, run, or taken exercise classes? What else have you done? How have you felt after aerobic activity? Make a note of your reflections below or on a separate piece of paper.

_____

_____

_____

_____

Unlike the other CAM interventions, which may or may not be for you, I urge you to include exercise in your Take-Charge plan. If it isn't yet part of your routine, start something. If it is, do you need to make it more regular or increase the intensity of your workouts? Check with your doctor to be sure that you can include this option, and then go easy at first, but don't avoid activity! Exercise is a powerful tool for taking charge of your emotional life.

RELAXATION TECHNIQUES AND GUIDED IMAGERY

Relaxation techniques and guided-imagery exercises are phenomenally effective in stopping anxiety because they sidestep the logical and analytic centers of the brain. In other words, these tools avoid the area that's involved in spiraling your worries out of control. Instead, they affect the sensory, emotion-based channels and bring about a direct and powerful calming response. These techniques also improve mood and decrease the amount of medication some people need to control their ADD symptoms.

You might want to pick up my *Stop Anxiety Now Kit* (available June 2007 from Hay House), which includes a guidebook and CD that teaches you how to use three of these self-soothing techniques:

1. Meditative relaxation
2. Progressive muscle relaxation
3. Guided imagery

Whether you use the kit or some other tool, I suggest you try all of these approaches. You may discover that one of them is especially appealing to you. Regularly use the one that suits you best.

MEDITATIVE RELAXATION RESPONSE

You've probably heard of Transcendental Meditation (TM) and may even have experience using it. It's one of the many techniques that brings forth the relaxation response; and it uses a specific, secret mantra. However, Herbert Benson, M.D., of The Mind/Body Medical Institute, has found a similar benefit when any sound, phrase, prayer, or mantra is paired with a quiet environment, a mental device, a passive attitude, and a comfortable position. When you meditate, you'll achieve calmness and relaxation by suspending the stream of thoughts that usually fill your mind. The process reduces stress and elevates your mood. While this is a wonderful option, please explore any meditative practices that appeal to you.

PROGRESSIVE MUSCLE RELAXATION

This technique involves a focused relaxation of all the muscle groups of your body. I usually start with the left hand, moving up the arm, across the shoulders to the head and neck, down the right arm, through the trunk, into the left thigh, down to the left toes, then on to the right thigh, and down to the right toes. I personally find progressive contraction and then relaxation of each muscle group to be the most effective way to promote tension release. I also find that it's best to work each muscle group two times.

There are many ways to relax your muscles in a progressive fashion. You can talk yourself through this exercise, or you can find a series of CDs that appeal to you. Once you discover something you like, use it regularly for a while and see what happens.

GUIDED IMAGERY

Guided imagery is a deliberate, focused sort of daydreaming: It uses words, music, and phrases to engage the imagination in creating a state of deep receptivity, calm, and inner peace. This technique is particularly beneficial for settling the nervous system and calming anxiety. Like meditative practices, it focuses attention and calms the mind, but it also works on the emotional part of the brain and skips over a lot of the talking and thinking areas.

Most people find guided imagery easier than meditation because it requires less focus and discipline. And because of the multisensory nature of the tool, they find it less difficult to hold their attention and absorb the images. While there's a lot of guidance available in tools, there's also plenty of space for finding yourself in the experience; it's a phenomenal balance.

Guided imagery has been found to increase levels of serotonin in the bloodstream—in other words, it works like an antianxiety or antidepressant medication, affecting the same chemical messengers that medicines such as Prozac, Paxil, and Luvox do. Guided imagery can be beneficial by itself, or it can be added to medication management for an increased effect.

While my *Stop Anxiety Now Kit* (available June 2007 from Hay House) contains a guided-imagery CD, there are many others on the market, and you'd do well to experiment with them. (I especially like the ones created by Belleruth Naparstek.) I suggest that you use such a tool daily for *at least* several months. You'll find that your ability to enter the experience increases exponentially over time, and the calming effect lasts for many hours after each use. Many people love this technique because it's an extremely effective tool to stop anxiety and improve mood.

For additional resources, visit:

- Academy for Guided Imagery: **www.academyforguided imagery.com**
- Health Journeys: **www.healthjourneys.com**
- The Healing Mind: **www.thehealingmind.org**

Please pause now to reflect on the role relaxation techniques and guided imagery might play in your Take-Charge program. What has your experience been with this realm of healing? What have you tried, and what has helped? Is this all new to you? What about it do you find appealing? Make notes of your reactions below or on a separate piece of paper.

_____

_____

_____

_____

You may have decided to explore or include a relaxation technique in your plan, or perhaps you're turned off by this realm right now—no matter. Whatever works for you is best for you.

MASSAGE

Massage has a long history. It was first written about in 2000 B.C. and is mentioned in ancient Egyptian, Persian, and Japanese texts. Hippocrates described its medical benefits, and the earliest Olympic athletes were treated with massage techniques prior to competitions.

According to the Centers for Disease Control's Advance Data publication number 343, May 2004, massage therapy involves pressing, rubbing and otherwise manipulating muscles and other soft tissues of the body. This causes them to relax, lengthen, and allow increased blood flow to the area. Using their hands, elbows, and feet, massage therapists may employ over 75 different methods—such as Swedish, deep-tissue, and neuromuscular massage and manual lymph drainage— to promote relief and healing.

This intervention has been used for symptomatic relief of anxiety, stress, depression, and ADD. *Massage Therapy Journal* did a wonderful piece titled "Massage Strategies for Depressed Patients" in the Fall 2003 issue. Dean Ornish also provides lots of examples of the healing power of massage in his book *Love & Survival.*

While I've never considered massage to be the whole answer to a psychiatric challenge, I do find that it routinely benefits my patients. Beyond diminishing anxiety and depressive symptoms, it provides a safe place to experience challenging emotions. You may recall that I mentioned studying massage therapy while in medical school. I love what it adds to the healing equation, and I'm driven to bridge the gap between Western medicine and these techniques. Today, I even write a regular column for *Massage Therapy Journal!*

Without knowing much about its benefits, many of us still feel drawn to this intervention. We might even say: "Wow, I really need a massage!" The soothing nature of the experience calms and heals our revved up systems. In fact, it's the most requested service in day spas!

For more information, visit:

- American Massage Therapy Association (AMTA): **www.amtamassage.org**

- Massage Magazine: **www.massagemag.com**

- National Certification Board for Therapeutic Massage and Bodywork (NCBTMB): **www.ncbtmb.com**

- Touch Research Institutes (TRI): **www.miami. edu/touch-research**

Take a few moments to reflect on the role massage might play in your Take-Charge program. What's your experience with it to date? Would you like to experiment with this ancient practice? Use the space on the next page (or a separate piece of paper) to record your thoughts.

You may have decided to get your first massage, add regular treatments to your schedule, or avoid this option all together. Whatever speaks to you is what you're meant to do.

LIGHT THERAPY

Do you feel better on a bright sunny morning or a cloudy, rainy one? Does the length of the day affect your mood? Are you more chipper in the summer than in the winter? Sunlight affects most people in powerful ways.

Many individuals who suffer from depression and bipolar disorder experience a seasonal variation in the severity of their problems. Perhaps you've heard of something called seasonal affective (*affect* means "mood") disorder or SAD. People with this condition usually experience either the onset of their depressions (or a worsening in the severity of their ongoing problem), in the fall and winter months, when the hours of daylight decrease and the strength of the sun's rays diminishes. Many of these folks get better if they sit in front of a bright light box every day; this is called "light therapy."

Recently, a study done in Denmark (*Acta Psychiatrica Scandinavica*, Aug. 2005, Klaus Martiny, M.D., Ph.D.) found that people with depressions *not of a seasonal variety* who were on antidepressant medication improved within one week when daily exposure to bright-white light of 10,000 lux was added to their treatment plan. The control group, who were on medication without bright light, didn't improve at the same rate. In addition, the benefit of light exposure wasn't confined to the winter months. Although the study was small and leaves a lot of questions unanswered, it highlights the importance of light in wellness.

Think back to your childhood. Do you remember your parents or teachers saying, "Go outside and play! It's a beautiful day. You shouldn't be indoors." That folk wisdom—that being in nature is heal-ing—has been passed from generation to generation.

While you may not need a light box in your life, you probably do need more time outdoors and more sun exposure (with sunscreen) than you currently get. Our spirits lift when we spend time in Mother Nature's playground.

I've always noticed that my moods are impacted by the weather. Having lived in the Northeast for most of my life, I was routinely more down in the dark times and up in lighter ones. My experience of mood and weather is common.

Just listen to the word choices of our language: We describe depressed periods as being dark, blue, or black and upbeat ones as bright spots. I now live in Tucson, Arizona, where it's bright and sunny almost all the time. Whenever I feel down, spending a half hour in the sun lifts my spirits. In order to prevent the down times from coming on at all, I try to enjoy time outdoors every day.

Take some time to think about your sunlight or light-box exposure. Do you get enough? What role might this option play in your Take-Charge program? Record your thoughts below or on a separate piece of paper.

_____

_____

_____

_____

For more information on light therapy, visit:

- The Cleveland Clinic Health Information Center: **http://www.clevelandclinic.org/health/health-info/ docs/1400/1484.asp?index=6412**

- Columbia University: **http://www.columbia.edu/~ mt12/blt.htm**

- The Mayo Clinic: **http://www.mayoclinic. com/health/seasonal-affective-disorder/MH00023**

Congratulations! You've now completed Step 4 of your Take-Charge course. As you create your own program from the steps we're covering, think synergistically. For example, might you want to meditate, exercise, or even sing outdoors in the sunlight? Would you do well to have a medical assessment, increase your medication dose, and begin a yoga practice?

Moving on, do you need to examine your life choices to see if some of your problems are the result of a poor fit between your nature and what you are trying to accomplish? In Step 5, you'll look at that "round-peg-in-a-square-hole" question and learn how healing is about honoring your gifts and respecting your limitations. Let's move into that area now!

STEP 5

Make Life Choices
That Fit Your Nature

Welcome to Step 5! I hope you're as excited as I am to be beginning this step. Here's where we get to start having fun together. From now on you'll be working in ways that are designed to access and nurture your core self. What could be more joyful than discovering and developing the wonder of you?

In Steps 1 through 4, you addressed the diagnostic and intervention issues necessary for building a healthy foundation for your Take-Charge structure. If you'd skipped or brushed past those chapters, the subsequent lessons of Steps 5 through 10 wouldn't work. You see, trying to access your inner wisdom, intrinsic capacity to heal, and ability to connect when you have an undiagnosed or untreated disorder is like constructing a building without a foundation. You can't really get anywhere, no matter how much you try. So even though slogging through diagnostic and intervention issues isn't the most fun, it's crucial and deeply liberating. Doing so opens the door to real pleasure because it allows you to step boldly into what makes you tick and sing.

So what's the lesson of Step 5? You have unique gifts and talents that you're meant to access, develop, and share with others. We all need what you have to offer. Similarly, you have your own distinct personality and way of being in the world, just as everyone does. Certain kinds of experiences, relation-ships, and environments will nurture you, while others will unsettle you. Whenever you operate from a connection to your essence and purpose, you'll feel at peace. But, being human, you have areas of limitation and challenge. If you ignore, disregard, or refuse to accept your nature and problems, and push yourself into places you don't belong, you'll experience discomfort and failure of some sort.

No one wants to do a bad job, be unsuccessful, or feel miser-able, but we all do sometimes. Whenever something's not working in your life, there's a reason for it; you are, in some way, disconnected from your essence and life path. But you can fix that. Perhaps you're unknowingly trying to fit a round peg into a square hole. You could be doing that in your choice of friends, lovers, or even career path.

In order to take charge of your emotional life, you need to identify and respect your nature, gifts, and challenges. In this chapter, you'll visit your passions and problems. You'll begin to consider your life choices in light of your growing wisdom, identifying what you can do to nurture what works for you and transform what doesn't. But before you begin, I'd like to share some stories that illustrate the lessons of this step.

THE IMPORTANCE OF SELF-KNOWLEDGE

In *There's Always Help; There's Always Hope,* I tell the story of two brilliant graduate students (who didn't know one another) who came to me with severe, major depression and a complete inability to function. One was in dental school, and the other was in a program in elementary education designed to create teachers. Both young women, who'd always done well academically, had begun failing their graduate-school course work. Then, seeing no way to succeed, each had become ill and unable to go forward.

You can read the details of their amazing journeys in my earlier book, but I want to share a key lesson of their stories with you now. Each of them had been unable to succeed because *she was pursuing something she wasn't meant to do.* And each of them was able to tri-umph upon finding and pursuing her proper path.

What do I mean by this? Well, as it turns out, the dental student had an unrecognized spatial learning disability. Her mind couldn't translate the flat images of teeth on x-rays into the three dimensions of the actual mouth. So, for example, she could never figure out which side of a tooth had the cavity. As a result of her limitation, a learning issue that couldn't be altered, she kept failing her lab courses. There was no way she could become a dentist.

When she'd originally decided to go to dental school, she didn't know how ill suited she was to that career. Once she got there and found herself unable to do the work, she became overwhelmed and depressed. By the time I met her, she was sick and devastated; she felt like a failure. Once the two of us identified her disability, she chose to switch to a more appropriate career path. She's now an accountant, and very successful in her work.

The elementary-education graduate student turned out to have undiagnosed ADD. Her brain chemistry made it impossible for her to balance the demands of maintaining order in a rowdy class and sticking with her lesson plan, so she kept failing her student-teaching course. Although she loved working with young kids, she couldn't handle them in a busy classroom, so she, too, became depressed. By the time I met her, she was ill and hopeless.

Once she and I identified her ADD and the mismatch of her career choice and her inborn limitations, she was able to forgive herself for failing. She decided to switch gears and work with children in a capacity that would fit her gifts and nature. She's now a pediatric nurse. She cares for one child at a time and loves her work!

So both women were unable to succeed and became sick when they tried to pursue careers ill suited to their gifts and limitations. Both were able to thrive upon discovering and pursuing paths more appropriate to their unique passions, talents, and challenges.

Pursuing Our Passions: My Story

We all have strengths, passions, and gifts; and we all have limitations, challenges, and hang-ups. Given our unique natures, we each feel comfortable in some situations and miserable in others. But we don't tend to honor our personalities or cut ourselves much slack. We often focus on our flaws and devalue our gifts, beating ourselves up when we don't like someone or feel that we don't fit in. We view those around us as better, more talented, or even perfect! We compare ourselves to others and neglect to see the whole picture. My patients often enact this dynamic with me. In their eyes, I'm flawless and they're failures.

The reason I look gifted is because I'm pursuing my passion and doing what I do well. I'm a healer, doctor, writer, connector, mom, wife, friend, speaker, and teacher. I've always been drawn to psychic pain and seen ways to help heal it; this comes naturally to me. I love hearing people's stories and stepping into their lives. I thrive on sharing myself with others and being in relationships. That's who I am and what makes *me* tick.

But I'm horrible when it comes to technology; and I also hate tension, conflict, and passivity. I'm the solve it, can-do peacemaker. I'm all there with anyone who wants to connect and work out issues, but I get unsettled by those who refuse to own their stuff and grow themselves. Furthermore, I recoil from computers. I know I have to use them, but they make me cuckoo! If I tried to be a programmer or engineer, I'd fail miserably. In fact, my aversion to technology could be a real hardship in today's world, but I don't let my limitation stop me.

I write my books, articles, and kits by pen, and then my beloved husband keyboards them for me! And if he couldn't do it, I'd find someone else who would. When I write, I need to feel the words flow from my brain and being, through my body, and into the tips of my fingers. I need to grasp my pen and hold it to the page. I have to physically *write* as I manifest my gift. I can't imagine being able to create with a keyboard, because it's just not me. It never has been and probably never will be either. Unbelievable, huh? But it's absolutely true: I'm deeply flawed and wildly successful!

I don't even like to use e-mail, because I want to see and hear you. I need to feel connected. I can't do what I do without human contact, and technology gets in my way. If I have the right setup, I can succeed. But if you were to put me in a cubicle with nothing but a computer, I'd probably become extremely depressed and unproductive. I need to be in relation and creation in order to be well.

I'm successful now because I've found my path, but I got fired from one of my first jobs, working in a furniture store, when I was 17 years old. When I hadn't learned what my trainer thought I should have mastered after three weeks, she showed me the door. To this day, I don't even know what I did wrong! But I learned something powerful from that experience: A paperwork- and sales-oriented desk job wasn't for me, and there was no way I was ever going to take another one. Neither the work nor the environment was right. I was meant to do something else—something that respected my nature, gifts, and significant limitations. I made it my business to figure out what that was.

Today, my work, family, social, and spiritual lives largely reflect who I am and what matters to me. But living authentically is an ongoing project; the work is never done. Life is about change, so I'm constantly tweaking, altering, and fine-tuning the mix. I expect to be doing that forever, but my building blocks are in place.

FINDING YOUR PATH

You, too, can become adept at identifying your nature, essence, gifts, passions, limitations, and areas of challenge. Using the right building blocks, you can create a big-picture plan that works for you. As you take charge of your emotional life, you'll learn to make choices that fit your unique and wondrous nature. Your inner wisdom is brilliant; you can access it and use it to make your life work.

So let's start to look at your story and the lessons of your journey. I've said that there's a path you're meant to travel that's uniquely yours, but what am I talking about? And how might you have gotten removed from living your own story? Let's go back to the beginning and see what we can discover together.

You were born with everything you need. You came with special gifts, intuitive wisdom, burning passion, and a particular purpose for entering this wondrous planetary sea of beings. You exited the womb ready to manifest your own special greatness, and those of us already here were waiting for you to arrive. This is a spiritual law of the universe.

But you were just a helpless baby, so you couldn't yet manifest all you were meant to become. You needed to be cared for, nurtured, and raised by grown-ups. You needed someone to hold, feed, and rock you—and to teach you the ways of the world. You needed this home, hearth, and help in order to survive, thrive, and prosper.

As a child, you were very much in touch with your essence, vibrancy, and passions. You were powerfully drawn to foods, people, and activities that resonated for you. You were equally put off by that which disinterested or unsettled you. But, like all children, you were driven by the need for approval, because when people thought well of you, they gave you the attention you needed in order to survive.

But in seeking that approval and taking on the beliefs and biases of those around you, some parts of yourself got squashed, shushed, pushed down, and ignored. Over time, as you continued to grow up, some of those key bits of your essence may have even become so secret that you stopped knowing they were there at all!

Like all of us, you learned to do some of what was expected of you, rather than all of what you might have been meant to do. Our parents and teachers unknowingly convey both growth-promoting and limiting lessons. Remember that song from the musical *South Pacific,* "You've Got to Be Carefully Taught"? As its lyrics remind us, we even learn whom to hate and fear from those who raise us. Given what we go through to get "growed up," many of us find it hard to know who we are or to believe that there's any value in being true to ourselves. But I'm here to tell you that there is, and to help you reconnect with who you are and what you're meant to do with your life.

As you work this step of your Take-Charge process, you'll find a series of exercises designed to help you connect with your essence, identify your limitations and life choices, and change the pieces of your plan that don't work for you anymore. Unlike Steps 1 through 4, Step 5 is much more action oriented. You'll be thinking, writing, reflecting, and examining your inner world as you seek your truth. If you draw, paint, sculpt, sing, or engage in any other art form, feel free to respond to the exercises below in your chosen medium.

So, let's start by identifying your gifts, passions, and other precious pieces. In your mind, go back in time to your early childhood and growing-up years. Without thinking too much, start filling in the blanks of the exercise below (or write your answers on a separate piece of paper).

Rediscovering Me

1. When I was a kid, I most wanted to give the world _____

    _____

2. My favorite things were (write down any associations that come to you; include the what and why):

a. Songs _____

b. Books _____

c. TV shows _____

d. Foods _____

e. Heroes _____

f. Friends _____

g. Relatives _____

h. Teachers _____

i. Subjects _____

j. Radio stations or programs _____

k. Colors _____

l. Games _____

m. Toys _____

n. Outfits _____

o. Seasons _____

p. Holidays _____

q. Hobbies _____

r. Movies _____

3. The best gift I ever got was _____

4. I could lose myself and all sense of time when I _____

    _____

5. I loved learning about _____

6. I was most joyful when I _____

7. My happiest memory is _____

8. I never minded _____

9. I could _____ for hours and not get bored.

10. I was really good at _____

11. My favorite folk or fairy tales as a child were _____

    _____ I especially liked the

    part when _____ because

    _____

12. The sayings that spoke (or still speak) to me include _____

    _____

    _____

13. Scenes that touched (or touch) me are _____

    _____

    _____

14. Art that moves me includes _____

    _____

15. Happiness is _____

16. Joy is _____

17. My secret dream is _____

18. I fantasize about _____

19. I know for sure _____

20. I love being _____

21. I am _____

22. If I were to make a treasure box and fill it up with what's most important to me (which could contain symbols of what matters), it would include _____

_____

23. If I had one day left to live, I'd want to _____

_____

24. When I was a kid, I wanted to be _____ when I grew up.

25. As a child, I imagined that as a grown-up, I _____

_____

26. The story I most like to tell about myself is _____

_____

27. I know that I am meant _____

28. My life wouldn't be complete if _____

_____

29. I am most grateful for_____

_____

30. My most moving life experiences to date include _____

_____

31. Even though I'm scared or doubtful, I know_____

_____

32. I'm living my passion when _____

33. I wish I could _____

34. Maybe I can _____

35. I'd love to be able to _____

36. If I were financially comfortable enough to do anything at all, I would _____

37. My private prayer is _____

38. I need to trust that I _____

Hopefully, you've now completed the "Rediscovering Me" exercise. If not, I urge you to give yourself the gift of doing it. Finding your personal right path requires you to fully step into the process, and the exercises in this chapter are designed to help you do that.

The premise behind the "Rediscovering Me" exercise is that somewhere in the back of your mind or deep within your soul, you know who you are, where you belong or fit, and what you're meant to be doing with your life. Given enough unencumbered space, you can begin to access your deep wisdom.

Reflect on your responses. What have you learned about what makes you tick and sing?

_____

_____

_____

_____

Now reflect on your life. How much does your life reflect what matters to you?

_____

_____

_____

_____

One way to get clarity about the fit between your essence and your life choices is to make two lists. In the first one, write down all the people, places, things, activities, and values that you hold dear. Rank them in order of importance to you, with number one being the most important, and so on.

Then make a list of all the ways you invest your energy and time. Think of a typical day, week, or month. How much time in a given week do you spend on each activity? List your involvements in order of energy spent, with number one being the most demanding, and so on.

In the ideal world, you'd be devoting the bulk of your energy or time to what's most important to you, and the numbers would line up between the two lists. If you find that your number one priority consumes the bulk of your time, and your next concern the second greatest amount of time, and so on, you're amazing and well on your way to wholeness!

Most people, however, find the comparison of their two lists to be far from ideal. But take heart, because you can only start from where you are. And by discovering the mismatch in your lists, you've identified your problems. This recognition and acceptance are the first steps in transforming your life.

Remember, Step 1 was about discovering and honoring the lessons of your story. If you think back to the questions you answered in that chapter, you probably recall considering these: *When in your life have you felt the best? The worst? What or who heals you? Unsettles you?* and so on. These queries were designed to get at the "right-fit" issue, and we're now looking at that topic from another vantage point.

Begin thinking about the mismatches between your two lists, or about the disconnects you've noted between your essence and life choices. You can actually fix some of the problems by simply identifying them and making a conscious choice to allocate your time differently. For instance, you may value your marriage more than your social life, but realize that you're spending more time hanging out with your work buddies than with your spouse. Simply cut down on activities with co-workers and plan more couple time into your week.

But what about the more complicated mismatches, or the confusion that lingers about who you really are? You may be concerned about the roadblocks you've encountered as you've tried to make your life reflect what matters to you the most. Are you worrying about your "stuckness"?

I'd like to tell you a story in order to show you how your answers to the questions in this step can help you find your own personal right path. While the road to authentic living may be long and tortuous, the actions you need to initiate in the Take-Charge process are straightforward and accessible. Read about Stan's journey to see what I mean.

DISCOVERING THE LOST SELF: STAN'S STORY

Many years ago, Stan, a 52-year-old technician in the casino industry, came to me for help. He was down on himself, addicted to stimulant drugs, and living with undiagnosed ADD. He'd always felt "less than," and actually believed that he was worthless. Although he could do his job well, he was working in a terrible setting for an addict looking to heal, and he didn't find his work especially fulfilling either.

I was troubled by Stan's self-assessment and worldview. Believing that all people have gifts, passions, challenges, and right fits and that his troubles had to be due to some mismatch, I urged him to tell me about his childhood and adult life. I wanted to know when he felt joyful, successful, empowered, and decisive, because his salvation depended on him accessing the essential pieces of himself and growing them. Without making a connection to his core being, Stan would have difficulty maintaining the hope and commitment necessary for doing the hard work of addiction recovery.

As my patient began to share his story, I learned that he was a gifted photographer, and he'd even previously had some professional success in pursuing his passion. But he'd come up against a brick wall when his career trajectory required him to be both organized and successful at self-promotion. Neither skill set came easily to him. On top of that, his undiagnosed ADD and addictive issues fed his problems. Without a better foundation (addressed in Steps 1 through 3) and major adjustments in the structure of his work, he couldn't succeed—but he didn't know that.

Seeing himself as a failure in business, Stan gave up on his love of taking pictures and entered the casino industry. By the time I met him, he'd been there for so many years that his other life was a distant memory.

I knew that this man was suffering because he was so disconnected from his core self. That split needed to be mended. I had to help him rekindle his inner flame, so I asked him to start bringing me samples of his photographic work.

Eventually, he did so, and they were great! I offered support and encouragement. I pushed him to clean out his darkroom, which had become a storage area, and to start using it again. After some time, he did that, too. As he immersed himself in the world of photography, be began to feel competent and joyful. The empowering energy that Stan generated by pursuing his gift enabled him to stay with the arduous process of therapy to take charge of his emotional life.

Stan and I worked together for a long time. We devoted the bulk of our effort to transforming his self-concept and worldview, combatting his addiction, and addressing his ADD. By the time he graduated from my care, he was much more self-confident. Although he was still working in the casino industry, he'd made photography a big part of his life. He ended his treatment feeling reborn.

Some years went by, and Stan and I lost touch with one another. Then my first book, *There's Always Hope; There's Always Help,* came out. While on a book and seminar tour, I reconnected with this patient when he came to one of my workshops. He was doing phenomenally well! He was clean and sober, having maintained his sobriety for nearly ten years. He'd recently saved up enough money to purchase a whole new set of photography equipment so that he could invest more fully in his passion. Empowered and clear about how to make his life work, he was elated and grateful. He'd come to thank me for helping him get back to knowing, trusting, and becoming who he was really meant to be.

Examine Your Past

You, too, can find and live your gifts; your answers are in your story. Think about Stan's journey, and then think about *your* adult life. Begin to identify your experiences of success, joy, fulfillment, or flow, as well as your episodes of challenge, disappointment, frustration, or personal failure. When have you felt most creative, empowered, and decisive in your life? What were you doing? Who was supporting you? In contrast, when have you felt the most demoralized, bored, confused, overwhelmed, and hopeless? What were you doing? Was anyone making it harder for you? Write your answers on the next page or on a separate piece of paper.

What tasks, skills, demands, and structures were part of each experience? Think about the details. What are your gifts or talents? What do you need to do to reclaim these pieces of yourself? How can you begin? What might you need to do to make sure your life choices fit your nature? (You may write your answers here or on a separate piece of paper.)

Now, think about stuckness. What's difficult for you? What do you need to do to address your difficulties? What sort of help might you need? What are you ready to take on? Commit to a plan and outline it in writing.

It might help you to hear more of Stan's story. You already know that he had to be willing to look to his history for answers about what he was meant to do. He had to commit to a long process of many tiny steps in order to transform his life. *But Stan also required medication, 12-step recovery-program tools, marital counseling, and psychotherapy in order to take charge of his emotional life.*

Would you do well to adopt some of those same techniques? Where are you, and why might you be stuck on your path to take charge of your emotional life? What should you do to get moving again?

You can't make life choices that fit your nature if you're trapped in one place, so let's examine some common reasons for this state. If you've hit a roadblock, there must be an explanation. Here are some possibilities. Which ones speak to you?

1. You have an undiagnosed or untreated condition that keeps you from being able to take charge of your emotional life.

2. You're trying to fit a round peg into a square hole.

3. You don't know what you ought to be doing.

4. You're afraid to trust what you know.

5. You don't feel entitled to live your story.

6. You're overwhelmed by the size of the project.

7. You're afraid of failure.

8. You devalue your gifts or magnify your limitations.

9. Your assumptions are faulty.

10. You're living a common definition of insanity: doing the same thing over and over again but expecting different results.

11. You haven't made yourself enough of a priority.

12. You're making progress but don't realize it.

13. You're impatient with yourself or the process.

14. You're a perfectionist.

15. You're actually there, but don't take the time to acknowledge the blessing of where you are!

As we explore each of these possibilities, look for yourself in the descriptions. Use the tips to overcome each of the roadblocks that you experience. Feel free to add in your own strategies as well.

1. You have an undiagnosed or untreated condition that keeps you from being able to take charge of your emotional life. As you know, this is a common reason for stuckness. Think of Stan's story or the tales we reviewed in Step 1. For example, depression makes it hard to get out of bed and concentrate; anxiety makes it difficult to think straight; ADD affects memory, concentration, focus, and level of interest; and mania makes it tough to sit still or remain on an even keel.

Tip: Whenever you're having trouble in your life, ask yourself whether you could be suffering from an illness, disorder, or hormonal issue that's compromising your capacity to be "in flow." Don't hesitate to seek help. Even if you're already being treated for something, the interventions may need to be changed, or you may have a second, unrecognized issue. Get help to get well!

2. You're trying to fit a round peg into a square hole. You probably recall that I experienced this mismatch when I tried to succeed in a paperwork/sales desk job. I was ill suited to the setting and work demands. Whenever we push ourselves to do something we aren't wired for, we'll become unsettled.

Tip: When you feel overwhelmed or frustrated, ask yourself: *Am I striving to do something that's wrong for me? Could I be trying to do the equivalent of running a marathon with a broken leg or singing in a chorus when I'm tone-deaf? Am I telling myself that I ought to be happy in this job, relationship, or outfit even though it's not really my thing?*

Be honest with yourself. If it feels wrong, there's a good chance that it is. Let yourself move on to something better suited to your nature and gifts.

3. You don't know what you ought to be doing. My experience is that most people say this when they're making the "meaning-of-life" question too big in their own minds. Every single person I've ever worked with can identify something that gives them pleasure and something that causes them pain.

Tip: Even if you need to start from the tiniest ember of light—such as knowing that you like to sing, dance, read, write, teach, do puzzles, or build things—you can begin to find your way. You need to fan the ember, create a big flame, and ignite the passion. You can do this by making time to pursue what appeals to you.

Start with a tiny effort and grow your investment until there's no question in your mind that you're in flow. Don't hesitate to experiment with various sparks until you find the ones that really glow for you; stay with the process. Your inner wisdom will guide you to the place where your light is meant to shine.

4. You're afraid to trust what you know. Many of us live in fear of stepping into our wholeness. The unknown is scary, and the devil we know seems somehow less troubling to us than the one we don't. But Franklin D. Roosevelt said it well: "The only thing we have to fear is fear itself." The worries we manufacture in our own heads are our biggest problem. We must take calculated risks if we're to take charge of our emotional lives.

Tip: Whenever you feel afraid, remind yourself of your power to prevail. Affirm: *I am meant to trust in my inner wisdom. My intuition is my guide. I owe it to myself to take on the challenges and rewards due me. I can prevail, and I intend to do so.*

5. You don't feel entitled to live your story. This is a common mantra, but it has no basis in the spiritual laws of the universe. You were put here for some reason that's unique to you, and the world needs your contribution.

Tip: When you start doubting your right to be you, talk back to your inner critic. Don't engage in a dialogue; just repeat a new belief over and over, creating a statement that works for you. I like this one: *I need to do what I am meant to do.* Or, *I exist to share my passion with the world.* Write your own mission statement, and say it whether you believe it or not. Doing so will empower you to live your own story.

6. You're overwhelmed by the size of the project. Most of us find that whenever we focus on the magnitude of a goal, we get overwhelmed. This is why, for example, 12-step recovery programs urge people not to think about giving up their addictive use forever. Their mottos "One day at a time" and "Keep coming back" speak to the need to start small and build from there.

Tip: Think in terms of the big picture and little steps. In other words, identify your goal, but focus on what you need to do *today* in order to get there. Remember the tortoise and the hare: Slow but steady won the race.

7. You're afraid of failure. One of my favorite lines about this subject is: "There are no failures, just slow successes." The most accomplished and fulfilled people on the planet have lived stories of setbacks, dead ends, mistakes, and adversities overcome. The only route to fulfillment is *through* the dread. Eleanor Roosevelt expressed this idea eloquently: "I believe that anyone can conquer fear by doing the things he fears to do."

Tip: Whenever you find yourself expressing fear, talk back to it. Say: *There are no failures; only slow successes. The way to conquer my fear is to take action—then my fear will melt away. I can and need to do this.*

8. You devalue your gifts or magnify your limitations. Many of us continue to believe that the grass is always greener on the other side of the fence. We agree with Groucho Marx and say, "I don't care to belong to any club that will have me as a member." But your talents are wondrous, and your challenges really do pale in comparison to them. It's not your essence that's the problem; it's what you're telling yourself about who you are that's tripping you up.

Tip: Focus on what you do well, figure out what's working in your life, and remind yourself of the good choices you've made to get to where you are. Or think of a challenge you've overcome, reminding yourself of your accomplishment. You can also come up with a way to nurture yourself in spite of your negative self-talk. How about a bath, a massage, or just a visit with a dear friend? You can begin to love yourself to wellness!

9. Your assumptions are faulty. Last week, a brave woman called me for advice during my weekly radio show. She shared her loss of joy and growing sense of helplessness, and she wondered what was wrong with her. Some years ago, in order to have more control of her time, she'd left her job to grow her own business. Now she was experiencing great success, but she was working 12 hours a day with no breaks! She'd made her life more unbalanced rather than easier, and she was feeling like a failure.

As we explored her situation, she said, "I made a lot of faulty assumptions when I decided to go this route."

I reassured her that we all do that sometimes, and we talked about the fact that her journey into entrepreneurship was meant to teach her something. She needed to discover the lesson and move on. She was overwhelmed, joyless, and depressed because it was time to change her course.

I said, "There's a reason you've gone this route. Your job is to figure out the lesson and take it with you into the next thing you do."

"Thank you," she responded. "I was feeling the same way. I guess I needed to hear it from someone else in order to acknowledge it."

Tip: If you're stuck, question your assumptions. Do you need to adjust your expectations of yourself or others? Should you cut your losses, learn your lessons, and move on? Perhaps you need to alter your beliefs about what will happen in order to be able to step into what comes next and beckons you. Assumptions can really hang you up, so challenge them!

10. You're living a common definition of insanity: doing the same thing over and over again but expecting different results. We all do this; it's a function of the way our minds work. Certain patterns become so ingrained in our neural circuitry that we replay them over and over. In other words, our brains become almost hardwired; they behave the way computers do. But of course, anytime we replay our situation, we get back the same old result. So, for example, if you keep going from one waitress job to another, and you get fired by your manager each time, then you're apt to get fired again—so maybe waitressing isn't your thing.

Tip: Look at your patterns. Do you see yourself reenacting the same problem over and over again, or even the same dialogue? If so, change at least one tiny piece of your behavior at a time and see what happens. Even small shifts can move mountains.

11. You haven't made yourself enough of a priority. Many of us neglect to put ourselves high enough up on the care list. But you can't succeed, thrive, grow, and give back if you're strung out and depleted. Taking charge of your emotional life requires time, energy, and other resources. Are you too busy taking care of everyone around you? Are you drained or depleted at the end of the day? How much of your schedule, energy, and money do you devote to your self-care, as compared to what you lavish on others?

Tip: Begin to examine your place on the priority list. Commit to treating yourself at least as well as you treat your friends, spouse, children, colleagues, pets, and even plants. Give yourself the best you have to offer. Only then will you accomplish what you're meant to achieve!

12. You're making progress but don't recognize it. This is one of the most common problems I see in my practice. We all focus so much on our limitations and what doesn't work in our lives that we neglect to see our gifts, growth, and progress. I spend a great deal of my clinical-care time reminding my patients of their own histories and accomplishments. It's striking to me that they invariably agree with my account and feel better after hearing it. I think about how much healthier we'd all be if we took the time to acknowledge and celebrate our own achievements.

Tip: Make it a point each day or week to reflect on your goals and small successes. Write them down in a journal and reread them periodically. You'll probably be amazed to discover how much you *are* changing.

13. You're impatient with yourself or the process. We live in a fast-paced, drive-through, shrinking world that's only getting more demanding, pressured, and frenetic. Gone are the days when you could get away and be truly inaccessible. We're expected to be consistently present, productive, and perhaps even superhuman. It's no wonder that we have unreasonable expectations of ourselves and tend to lose patience quickly. We expect a quick fix and feel like failures when our growth and transformation process follows its slow but steady course. But significant progress takes tons of time. We must hang in there if we're to achieve our goals.

Tip: Remind yourself that nothing worth striving for comes easy. In fact, if your journey doesn't feel slow, arduous, and frustrating, you're probably cutting necessary corners. Tell yourself that you're not in a race to the finish; you're meant to savor your travels and relish the pauses. You need breaks and downtime!

14. You're a perfectionist. So many of us are! If you're expecting yourself to be perfect, it will be hard for you to effect change, because it's difficult to build on your accomplishments when none of them are good enough for you. And it's tough to take risks and step into the unknown when you're expecting yourself to do a perfect job. That goal is too big for any human being. No one is perfect; to err is to be human. We're all a little broken, limited, flawed, and challenged. In fact, our vulnerabilities are often what's most appealing about us!

Tip: Tell yourself, *My best is good enough. Perfection isn't the goal. To err is to be human.*

15. You're actually there, but don't take the time to acknowledge where you are! We seem to believe that we haven't taken charge of our emotional lives if we still have work to do. But being alive involves facing and negotiating challenges every day. If you have your building blocks in place, you're in charge! You may regularly need to reorganize the pieces, but as you make life choices that fit your nature, you'll be "there" in an ongoing way.

Tip: Regularly ask yourself, *Am I making life choices that fit my nature?* If the answer is yes, celebrate. If no, then make the changes necessary to get to yes. You can live the life you were meant to lead—you might even be doing so already!

As you conclude your Step 5 work, let's review what you've learned. You now know that you're genetically and spiritually endowed with gifts and challenges, and you're meant to identify and honor both in your efforts to take charge of your emotional life. You've called forth some of your essential pieces—those embers, sparks, or even the internal flames that give your life meaning. You've explored mismatches between your true self and your life choices and chosen to implement some steps and strategies to better align your being with your doing. You may even have decided to explore medical or psychological assessment, counseling, coaching, or therapy.

I urge you to invite in all the supports you need in order to work your Take-Charge program. Guides and mentors are crucial in healing. We often benefit from the voice and insight of others.

That said, we also have an amazing capacity to self-heal. We carry around a lot of beliefs that imprison us. Given enough guidance in identification and transformation of our self-destructive brain circuits, we can actually learn how to reprogram some of our negative self-talk loops on our own. And even if we can't do it *all* alone, we can (and need to) do a lot of self-talk to take charge.

In Step 6, you'll discover how to identify the learned beliefs that imprison you. You'll master some cognitive-behavior techniques that you can use to transform your stuck-in-a-rut thinking and take charge of your emotional life.

STEP 6

Identify the Beliefs That Imprison You, and Reprogram the Brain Circuits Involved

Welcome to Step 6! The premise behind this chapter is that what you believe—what you tell yourself both consciously and unconsciously—affects what happens in your life. We might even say that you actively *create* your own world. Although you may not recognize your power, you do wield it. And with enough persistence, you can identify the beliefs that imprison you. You can then develop powerful mind-body tools to reprogram those negative mental circuits. Using those strategies, you'll literally change your brain to change your life.

How can you possibly have so much power? You probably doubt that you do, and you may be thinking, *If I had that, I would be using it to make my life better, easier, and more fulfilling. What person in their right mind would choose the pain and suffering I experience? You can't possibly be right.*

Well, you wouldn't consciously create distress for yourself, but you do so without knowing it. You see, we all carry around internalized messages, ideas about ourselves and others. Some of them are healing, and others harm us. We're aware of some of those beliefs because of the chatter we hear in our heads, but are unaware of many others, in spite of their power.

You learned most of those lessons early in your development and stored them away without realizing it. But your internalized messages affect the course of your life. The healing ones are encouraging, gentle, loving, optimistic, honest, and fair; the harmful ones are critical, discouraging, pessimistic, and harsh. Your ideas determine your behavior and what the universe gives you back in response. But how do you acquire these beliefs? How is it that they affect you as they do, and how can you change them?

THE ORIGINS OF SELF-CONCEPT

Well, the lessons we learn about ourselves in childhood determine our self-concepts as adults. The models you were exposed to or taught during your formative years dramatically affect your mind-set. For most of us, our primary learning laboratory is our family of origin. We learn how to think about ourselves and others from what our parents teach us by word and example.

Although our teachers, classmates, and religious leaders may exert powerful developmental influences on us as well, we experience the messages contained in our "home base" as the most powerful. Obviously, if you were raised in an environment other than a traditional family with two parents, then you were exposed to messages and models of a different nature. The home environment has the greatest power to affect the mind-set of a developing child, whatever form it takes.

As children, we learn and store away information with the degree of cognitive development that we have at the time of the event. For example, if we're young and still very concrete or literal in our thinking, we may simply store away a lesson such as "I am a bad boy" or "I am a naughty girl." Since our capacity to understand what might make a person good or bad hasn't yet been developed, we store the information as a simple fact.

Without being consciously aware of these stored self-concepts, we're influenced by them throughout our adult lives. Since these old messages can cause dysfunction and intense pain, we may find ourselves questioning our ideas and choices enough to identify some of our negative core beliefs over time. Having figured out what they are, we can use our adult ideas to talk back to our childlike ones. By recognizing and subsequently challenging our internalized beliefs, we can change and replace them with more constructive and positive notions. This healing process involves using a cognitive-behavior technique, a form of self-talk called "affirmations," to reprogram destructive thoughts. You'll learn more about that later in this chapter.

But before discovering how to change the mind-set, we need to ask: *How do those negative lessons actually affect us? What do we do with them? What does it really mean to be influenced by our past?*

MARKING TIME

Strange as the idea may seem, we all reexperience our pasts in the present as we tell ourselves what we learned. Having been called stupid or lazy in childhood, we may tell ourselves the same things now. We also hear our self-concepts and worldviews reflected back in the words of others, even when those people aren't actually saying those words. So we may "hear" our friends or bosses calling us dumb or unmotivated, when they're simply following up with us to determine where we are with a project.

Additionally, we re-create familiar family dynamics in our adult relationships, even if the original situations were (and often still are) painful to us. We may pick critical friends, bosses, lovers, and life partners. What's familiar somehow feels right, hence the popular notion that "women marry their fathers" and "men marry their mothers."

In spite of our adult desires to experience joy, fulfillment, and pleasure in our relationships and pursuits, we often unknowingly re-create the pain, sadness, and loss of our childhoods. We do it minute to minute by what we tell ourselves, and year after year as a result of the choices we make. Our biggest challenge can be trying to figure out how to live the life we're meant to have, as opposed to the one someone else might have taught us.

You've probably heard the expression "You're your own worst enemy." I believe this statement to be true. We are, in many ways, what we believe. Both my personal life and clinical work with patients have shown me how frequently our troubles are the result of self-sabotage. We often impose limits on ourselves that trap us into what doesn't work. Until and unless we challenge our beliefs, we remain stuck in unproductive, even self-destructive, positions.

Breaking Free from Our Misconceptions

I'm going to give you a silly, simple example of what I mean by staying trapped by an idea. A long time ago when my now-teenage son was three years old, he and I had a battle of wills about vegetables! I'd made dinner, and we were sitting down to eat. Gabe announced that he didn't like broccoli (having never eaten it before) and refused to sample it.

I insisted that he try one bite, and if he disliked it, he could have a substitute. He refused to do so. He was given multiple chances to challenge his belief and cooperate. But even knowing that his rigidity would land him in bed without any further dinner, treats, or bedtime story, he refused to try the broccoli. He was eventually carried off to his room, kicking and screaming.

Gabriel was a stubborn little boy, but I was even more determined than he was when it came to health issues. So when we sat down to green beans the next evening and he pulled the same routine, he was carried off to bed as he had been the night before. This went on for four days, with Gabe insisting each night that he didn't like the vegetable on his plate, no matter what it was. It didn't make a difference if he'd never tasted it before, or if he'd eaten it with gusto in the past.

Finally, on the fifth night, we sat down to broccoli again. The familiar routine began to play itself out until just before the trip to bed. Then, wonder of wonders, Gabe lifted the tiniest spear of broccoli to his mouth and put it in. And guess what? His reluctant face broke into a smile. He finished that first piece, and as he was stabbing the second one with his fork, he said "I like broccoli! Can I have some more?"

"Of course, Gabe," I answered. "But wouldn't you have saved yourself a lot of upset if you had just tried the broccoli the first time?" He nodded.

"There's a lesson here," I said. "Don't insist you know something when you don't know for sure that it's true. Your stubbornness will only cause you grief. Other people might even get angry with you, and do or say things that upset you. It's best to be open-minded and willing to try new things. Do you agree?"

By now Gabe was on his third helping of broccoli. He nodded again and said, "I don't know why I wouldn't try it, Mom. But I learned my lesson."

I believe that he did learn to challenge his stuck thinking. In fact, we never had an argument like that again—not about anything! What a relief that was to all of us in the family.

Now this may seem like a silly story about a three-year-old child and vegetables. But is it really so irrelevant? Have you ever enacted this kind of dysfunction in your adult life? For instance, have you ever insisted that someone didn't like you, that you couldn't accomplish a goal, or that your input wasn't valued when you didn't know for sure that you were correct? I doubt that you can truthfully answer no to this question.

We all fall into "stinking thinking" sometimes. And when you get stuck in one of those ruts, what happens? You act on the basis of your assumption. You treat the person whom you believe doesn't like you in a way that may actually lead them to feel that way. You shy away from pursuing goals that you believe you can't achieve, so you never meet them. Or you keep your mouth shut, thinking that no one values your input, and thus lose the opportunity to have any say in what happens to you. Your beliefs can get you into a lot of trouble. In fact, what you think can alter the course of your life.

UNEARTHING DESTRUCTIVE ASSUMPTIONS

Some of your counterproductive thoughts are easy to identify, while others are deeply buried. The ideas that are readily accessible are the ones that you hear in your head. For instance, your internal voice might say, *That was a stupid thing to do* or *You're such a loser.* You can discover these perceptible beliefs by attending to the dialogue in your mind. But identifying your more deeply buried assumptions requires more digging. It involves examining your destructive life patterns and tracking their origin. What did you learn that you're unconsciously playing out? You need to do some detective work to discover the underlying beliefs that you haven't as yet given voice to. Let's look at some examples of each scenario—accessible beliefs and buried ones—so that you get a handle on what I mean.

Reworking Accessible Beliefs

If you think back to Stan's story, you'll recognize the thought that imprisoned him. Remember when he hit a wall in his photography business? He told himself that he couldn't succeed in that line of work. The idea *I can't do photography for a living* led him to give up on his passion and take a job in the casino industry.

With a lot of time and help, Stan was able to challenge his belief and rediscover his inner flame. In this case, his counterproductive thought was relatively easy to identify. But since so many of his life choices had followed from it, the reprogramming effort involved a lot of work.

What about a more simple example of a destructive belief—one that's easily identified, challenged, and reprogrammed? Well, my patient Sam was a particularly anxious fellow who tended to expect the worst possible outcomes to problems. One day he came in overwrought because his boss hadn't responded to voice-mail or e-mail communications about a pressing work matter. Sam was convinced that he'd made some fatal error, that his boss was avoiding him as a result, and that his job was in jeopardy. He was afraid to go back to work. "I'm about to be fired," he insisted tearfully.

But Sam actually excelled at his work. His performance reviews were routinely exceptional. In fact, he'd just been given a glowing evaluation! I reminded him of his workplace history and challenged him to consider alternative reasons for his boss's lack of response. As he began using his rational brain to challenge his dysfunctional belief, he was able to settle down.

Armed with a list of possible causes for the situation, Sam chose to change the belief that told him, *I'm in serious danger whenever someone is slow to respond to my questions.* Instead, he decided to say, "Not everyone responds as quickly as I do when queried. I need to tell myself: *Calm down. No news is good news. If I'm at risk, I will surely be told about it.*"

Sam committed to making these few sentences a new mantra, and he repeated them in his head all the way back to work. When he got there, he discovered the reason for the silence—his boss had the flu!

I continued to work with Sam for several months. Occasionally, he'd start to express that old, crippling belief. But before he even finished the sentence, he'd stop himself and state: "I don't know why I'm saying that, because I know it's old thinking. No news is good news. If I'm at risk, I'll surely be told about it."

By changing his mind and reprogramming that dysfunctional pattern, Sam's anxiety progressively diminished. Empowered to take charge of his emotional life in a new way, he was able to graduate from my care.

Reworking Hidden Beliefs

Now let's look at an example of someone with a deeply buried but disabling belief. I'd like to tell you about Melissa, who came to me hoping to heal her romantic life. Her marriage had ended some years before when her husband shared his infidelity and desire to repartner with his lover.

Melissa was devastated. "Perhaps I haven't fully recovered," she said, "because I shy away from romantic relationships. And whenever I do get involved with someone, I hold myself way back. Eventually he always leaves. It becomes a replay of my marriage experience."

The two of us got down to work, trying to sort out the lessons of Melissa's history. What did she believe, and why was she replaying an abandonment dynamic over and over again? As it turned out, she came from a family with a disabled sibling. She was a good student and a quiet child, and her parents didn't recognize the attention she needed in order to thrive. She was often expected to take care of her brother, having to put aside her schoolwork and whatever else she wanted to do. As a result, Melissa learned the lesson: *My needs aren't important; I have to help those less fortunate, no matter what the cost to me.* Although she was somewhat aware of this conviction, she didn't recognize its influence.

When it came to relationship issues in her adult life, that internalized idea exerted its silent power. During Melissa's courtship, she often played the role of silent caretaker, putting up with and even accommodating her then-fiancé's troubling behavior. When he proposed, her inner-wisdom voice said *Don't do it!* but her dysfunctional belief countered with *You can't hurt his feelings. He's a nice enough guy. He needs you. You have to say yes.* Without recognizing that the childhood message *My needs aren't important; I have to help those less fortunate* was at play, she said yes.

Upon entering the marriage, Melissa buried her inner wisdom along with her turmoil and misgivings. She tried to make things work, but out of sight and mind is not out of life. In spite of her efforts to build a loving partnership, she couldn't alter what she'd known to be true: Her husband wasn't ready and wouldn't fully commit to the union.

When he left, Melissa was devastated. She didn't remember that she'd had her own misgivings from the very beginning. She personalized his decision that she wasn't good enough for him, and then carried this sense of low self-worth into subsequent relationships, dating unavailable men who'd never commit enough to hurt her so deeply again.

It took Melissa and me months to identify the crippling belief that had been behind her acceptance of the marriage proposal. By looking at her childhood, we finally figured out where the idea had come from. Armed with this knowledge, we began to reprogram the self-destructive brain circuit.

As an adult, Melissa understood the importance of caring for herself and her own needs in life. She came to recognize that she'd abandoned herself in choosing to enter a marriage that wasn't meant to be. The demise of the union was inevitable. *She* was good enough, but she'd made the wrong choice. *It* wasn't right! She'd set herself up to suffer when she ignored her inner wisdom and enacted the learned belief. She'd put her own needs aside to avoid "hurting his feelings." As a result, she unknowingly hurt herself.

Her internal script needed to be rewritten. It became: *My inner wisdom is my guide. I need to honor my feelings, give them a voice, and act on them. I am meant to silence the voices telling me that I don't count. Those aren't really mine. I am good enough, and I deserve to experience joy.*

Melissa and I worked together for some time. She needed to develop skill in identifying and heeding the wisdom of her inner voice, ferreting out and challenging the old belief and living more authentically. Throughout her work, she repeated the new script she'd created. This exercise enabled her to reprogram the old tape as she strove to believe what she now knew to be true. She graduated from my care several years ago, feeling empowered and transformed.

The universe acts in synergistic and strange ways sometimes. When I wrote down Melissa's story, I hadn't heard from her in quite a while. We'd connected perhaps two or three times since her graduation. Yet, as I was writing *about* her, she was writing *to* me. Within days of completing this passage, I received a New Year's greeting card from her. She'd just read my first book and loved it. She was writing to tell me that, and to let me know how well she was doing. She was engaged to a wonderful man, and she'd truly reprogrammed her mind and changed her life. She was grateful and delighted to have me share this story of her transformation in order to help you.

THE POWER OF YOUR MIND

We've now covered three examples that demonstrate the power of beliefs to affect life paths, and I'm sure you resonated with some elements of each story. What struck you? To whom do you relate the most—Gabe, Sam, or Melissa? Have you ever engaged in an effort to reprogram your destructive beliefs? How well did you do?

Perhaps you have some experience with affirmations or other cognitive-behavior techniques. These methods are extremely powerful in altering problematic brain circuits, because they work by creating new neural pathways. You see, when you tell yourself something over and over, the same pattern of neurons fires repeatedly. Eventually, that circuit takes on a life of its own. So when you encounter the familiar situation, your brain begins to tell you what it already knows (almost without thinking). After feeding yourself something negative for years, such as *My needs aren't important,* your mind has that thought pretty well fixed in place.

But you can change this! The way to do so is by telling yourself something different over and over again until *it* becomes ingrained. You don't have to think the new message is true for it to take; you just have to keep saying it. After a while, it will become fixed enough that you'll believe it instead.

There's something else I need to teach you about the strength of your thoughts to affect your life. It concerns the minute-to-minute power of your mind-body connection. Whenever you give yourself encouraging or positive messages, internal chemicals are released that calm the deep limbic system of your brain. This makes you feel happy and relaxed.

By contrast, when you focus on sad, angry, worrisome, or critical thoughts, your brain releases chemicals that activate your deep limbic system and make you feel tense, anxious, and unsettled. So even before you reprogram your problematic circuits, you can harm or heal yourself by what you allow your mind to say.

LOOKING INWARD

In the remaining pages of Step 6, you'll identify the beliefs that imprison and harm you. You'll then develop strategies to bring about both immediate relief and long-term change. The first part of this process involves figuring out what thoughts you need to alter . . . and perhaps you know some of them already. If so, write them on the lines below or on a separate piece of paper:

_____

_____

_____

Most imprisoning thoughts are the result of fear, self-devaluation, guilt, pessimism, overgeneralizing, and "catastrophizing" (or expecting the worst). Let's look at each of these categories a bit to help you find your inner demons.

— **Fear** is a big issue—in fact, it can cripple the most mighty! As I mentioned earlier, according to Franklin D. Roosevelt, the only thing we have to fear is fear itself. That's how prominent this force is in our lives. In fact, it's the greatest cognitive distorter. We can't think straight when we're anxious. We may worry about our health, our financial security, the strength to endure challenges, or the ability to perform at an acceptable level. We might be afraid of flying in an airplane, losing our keys, or driving our car in snowy conditions. We may dread abandonment, abuse, annihilation, or failure. These are just a few examples.

What are you afraid of? Is this an area of stuck thinking for you? What do you say to yourself?

— **Self-devaluation** is very common in negative thinking. You might enact this by labeling or calling yourself names, for example: *I'm a failure and a jerk.* Or perhaps you devalue yourself by comparing yourself unfavorably to others: *I'm not as smart as Sally, or as funny as Jon.* You might even put yourself down by overgeneralizing (which you can also do with fear, guilt, and the like): *I'll never be promoted, I'm always left out;* or *No one will be interested in my ideas.* I often hear the ultimate self-devaluation from my patients. It sounds like this: *I'm not enough, I don't matter; The world would be better off without me;* or *I'm a burden to those around me.*

How do you devalue, criticize, label, or belittle yourself? What do you say?

— Let's move on to **guilt**. We feel this emotion when we neglect to say or do something that we believe we *should* do, or when we do or say something that we think we *shouldn't*. Whenever the word

121

should comes into your mind, you're holding yourself to someone else's standard. Often, you're articulating a rule of behavior that you learned while growing up. Think back to Melissa's story. She learned to put herself second, and that felt right. So she said to herself, *I should accept this marriage proposal. My feelings aren't important. I can't hurt him.*

Guilty thoughts can also surface when people survive disasters that take or destroy the lives of others around them. This is called survivor guilt, and may sound like this: *It should have been me.* You might also feel guilty for outperforming your siblings or parents: *I shouldn't have embarrassed them or shown them up;* or for failing to meet the expectations of others: *I should have stayed in that marriage. My parents loved my ex-spouse.*

Finally, you may even feel guilty when someone else criticizes or hurts you. You could be enacting an old dynamic and assuming that you're responsible for the other's behavior. The thinking is: *I shouldn't have said or done what I did. I regret my behavior.*

What's the role of guilt in your internal dialogue? How often do you find fault with yourself for what you should have done but didn't, or what you shouldn't have done but did? What do you say to yourself?

———————————————————————————————————————

———————————————————————————————————————

———————————————————————————————————————

— **Pessimistic thinking,** seeing the cup as half empty instead of half full, is a powerful warden. It can imprison you and forever keep you from taking charge of your life. Studies looking at how well children learn when teachers are told that their students are bright versus intellectually limited demonstrate that the way the instructors *view* the pupils—whether it's accurate or not!—determines classroom performance. Smart kids who are treated as if they're limited do poorly; average children approached with high expectations perform extremely well.

Think about the implications of this: If you expect yourself to fail, you most likely will. Additionally, if you expect others to treat you poorly, or if you think that unpleasant things are going to happen, you'll search for and find the negative outcome. Each time you do so, you'll reinforce your belief that the world is a big, bad, or scary place. You'll withdraw more and more, and take less and less charge of your life.

But we're imperfect beings who live in a flawed world. Perfection can't be the goal. Every single moment is full of opportunities and problems, blessings and curses. You can choose to focus on the negative and *feel* bad or on the positive and *feel* good. For example, during a wonderful celebratory meal, you can let a chipped plate destroy your pleasure in the company and wonderful food. Or at the theater, you can permit the occasional distraction of someone coughing in the audience to diminish your enjoyment of the play. When your co-worker calls in sick and your workload increases for the day, you can tell yourself, *I bet she won't be in for weeks and I'll be overwhelmed* or *Thank heaven I'm well and can manage the extra work for today.* Which thought do you believe will make for a better day?

Are you pessimistic at times? When do you expect the worst for yourself or others? What do you say in your head?

_____

_____

_____

— We all **overgeneralize** at times, and whenever we do, we set ourselves up. When we use words such as *always* and *never,* we're falling into this trap. Telling ourselves *I'll never get promoted, I'll always be abandoned,* or *No one could possibly love me* is a recipe for staying stuck.

Similarly, saying *I can't change my life, You never listen to me,* or *Everyone is out to get me* keeps us stuck. Nothing in life is absolute. When we make global statements, we leave no space for growth, options, or creativity. Taking charge of your emotional life requires you to follow a unique path specific to your challenges and gifts. You can only find your way if you are open-minded and flexible in your thinking.

In what ways do you overgeneralize? Is it mostly when thinking about yourself, others, or both? What do you actually say?

————————————————————————————

————————————————————————————

————————————————————————————

— Perhaps the most crippling series of thoughts emerges when we **catastrophize**. In this behavior, both fear and pessimism come together, and we assume the absolute worst. For example:

- Our spouse is late, so we say, *He must be dead.*

- When our friend needs to talk, we decide, *He's chosen to end the relationship.*

- Upon receiving a letter from the IRS, we believe, *I'm going to be imprisoned.*

The excessive fear that accompanies catastrophizing unsettles our nervous systems in dramatic ways, and we feel absolutely awful. At this point, we're often unable to take action of any kind.

When do you catastrophize? What's the fear behind your thoughts? What do you tell yourself?

————————————————————————————

————————————————————————————

————————————————————————————

BEGINNING TO CHANGE YOUR MIND

Now that you've done some thinking about the beliefs that imprison you, it's time to get into the real work of Step 6: identifying and reprogramming your dysfunctional thoughts. You've already written down some of your problematic beliefs as you read through the examples, descriptions, and questions in this chapter. What other ones might you be carrying?

You'll be cataloguing all your counterproductive beliefs later in the chapter by completing "My Negative-Thought List." In preparation, think about your areas of success and challenge. What ideas may have contributed to your difficulties? Write them down on your list. You may have 3 statements, or you may have 22. Remember to include your experiences of fear, self-criticism, guilt, pessimism, overgeneralizing, and catastrophizing.

To help you identify more negative thoughts, do the following "Sentence-Completion Exercise." As you go through it, write down whatever comes into your mind without thinking about it. Just let what's in there pop up. You may be surprised by what's revealed to you when you create this opportunity.

SENTENCE-COMPLETION EXERCISE

I am _____

I can't _____

Men _____

Aging _____

Women _____

Children _____

Other people _____

Death _____

God _____

Money _____

No one _____

Sickness _____

Everyone _____

Sex _____

Love _____

Anger _____

Sadness _____

Loss _____

Forgiveness _____

Life _____

Hope _____

Now read your completed sentences, putting a mark next to those that you recognize as imprisoning beliefs. Include them in your Negative-Thought List.

My Negative-Thought List

1. _____

2. _____

3. _____

4. _____

5. _____

6. _____

7. _____

8. _____

9. _____

10. _____

Visualization for Healing

Before I teach you how to reprogram your imprisoning beliefs, I'd like you to pause and do a visualization exercise with me.

Imagine an all-powerful, all-knowing, loving, compassionate, and caring being beside you. Allow yourself to see, hear, smell, feel, and fully sense the presence of this wise entity, and get comfortable. Breathe deeply into the moment. Perhaps you'd like to hold hands with this visitor or get close in some other way. Your guest is your helper, protector, assistant, and co-healer. It may be someone you already know, or someone who's coming to you for the first time.

In the presence of this wise being, read your negative thought list aloud. Allow your co-healer to feel concern for you. Let yourself recognize the pain your wise friend experiences as you voice your harmful beliefs. Invoke compassion for yourself as you sit with this pain for some moments.

Then open your heart and mind as widely as you possibly can. Repeat the following affirmations out loud three times:

- *I am at one, at peace, and at ease.*
- *I have all that I need.*
- *I am safe, abundant, blessed, and wondrous.*
- *I carry the mystery and beauty of the infinite within me.*
- *I am lovable and loved.*
- *I am more than enough.*
- *I am meant to be.*

These words come from your wisdom healer. As you repeat them, recognize the peace that descends upon you and your guide simultaneously. Feel the soothing chemicals suffuse your brain and body, and allow yourself to relax fully into this healing. You're at one, at peace, and at ease. You want for nothing.

Sit with the blessings of these affirmations for as long as you wish, repeating the words that touch you. Feel them cushioning you, comforting you, and forming a protective energy field around you. Let your body and spirit relax deeply into this safe space. Stay there as long as you wish, and know that you can return to this place anytime that you want. It's always there for you.

TRANSFORMING NEGATIVE SELF-TALK

Now that you're calm, it's time to start developing positive, affirming thoughts to speak back to your internal critic. This exercise involves taking each negative idea on your list and fashioning an uplifting antidote in response.

How do you decide what sort of statements to create? Well, following are some guidelines:

1. All affirmations need to be in the present tense. So let's say that the negative statement on your list is *I'm a failure.* Rather than saying *I will be successful,* you might try *I am successful* or *My best is good enough.*

2. Write statements that are positive rather than negative. For example, if your imprisoning thought is *No one will ever love me,* your antidote might be something such as *I am lovable and loved,* as opposed to *I am not going to be abandoned.*

3. Your validating statement doesn't need to be believable to you at this moment. In fact, it probably won't be or you wouldn't have to create and say it. The affirmation is something you choose to say now in order to bring about changes in your belief system and in what comes to you in the future as a result.

Let's practice this exercise. Take your list of negative thoughts and start writing positive antidotes for each one. Here are some examples:

*   "I'm fat and ugly" **becomes** *My body serves me well,* or *I appreciate the miracle of my body.*

*   "I can't take care of myself" **becomes** *There's always help; there's always hope.*

*   "People are scary" or "The world is unsafe" **becomes** *I am at one, at peace, and at ease. The universe provides for me.*

*   "I won't be happy until I have financial security" **becomes** *I am comfortable and safe. Abundance is mine for the asking.*

*   "I'm a nobody" **becomes** *I am a blessed child of the universe.*

*   "I'm weak" **becomes** *I am vibrant, energetic, and empowered.*

- "I'm alone" **becomes** *I am held in the warm embrace of the infinite.*

- "I should be more outgoing or friendly" **becomes** *I am wonderful just as I am.*

- "I'm scared" **becomes** *My Lord is with me. I do not fear.*

- "My anxiety will escalate out of control" **becomes** *I have tools to use to interrupt my anxiety.*

- "I am destined to fail" **becomes** *I create my own destiny, and I choose to succeed.*

Sometimes finding the proper affirmation or antidote to a self-imprisoning thought takes a while. Don't get discouraged. Instead, sleep on it, get help, and experiment. The right answer will be revealed.

Once you've created affirmations for each of your negative ideas, write these positive statements on index cards. These will become your reprogramming tools. But how are you to use them? Each morning and evening, you are to take three deep belly breaths, thank the universe for giving you the power to heal, and then read the statements on your cards. Say each one out loud three times before going on to the next, letting the words sink into your being. When you're finished, thank the universe again for supporting you, and then go on with your day.

It's crucial that you read your affirmations regularly. Remember, you're up against entrenched ideas. Each time you affirm yourself, you'll feel the immediate, self-soothing benefits. Over time, you'll alter your mind-set loops and dramatically change your life.

A Powerful Transformation: Carol's Story

You may doubt my words. Perhaps you're thinking: *I can't really change my life by choosing to say stuff I don't even believe. Affirmations can't do that much to make a difference. That's magical thinking!* I'd like to share one of the most dramatic tales I know in order to demonstrate the power of your mind, the effect of affirmations and visualizations, to change your body and your life's course.

Some years ago I attended a Women in Leadership conference in San Francisco that was sponsored by Leadership, Inc. One of the speakers was a runner who described how she used her mind to qualify for the Olympics when a serious year-long injury prevented her from training for the team tryouts.

Since I unfortunately can't remember the name of the speaker, I'll call her Carol. She was a schoolteacher who ran track, a fast and gifted athlete whose dream had always been to qualify for and compete in the Olympic Games. So one year before the tryouts (which come up every four years), she chose to take 12 months off from her job, rent a home adjacent to a track, and devote her time to training for the qualifying races.

Soon after she moved into her new home, she injured her leg very seriously. As I recall, she tore some ligaments. She was unable to even walk, and was told that the recovery process would take a year. Perhaps she'd be able to run by the end of that time, but she surely couldn't train for the Olympics. It was unlikely that she'd be able to run by the tryout date!

Carol was devastated. As she hobbled around on her new crutches, she felt the hopelessness wash over her. *What will I do now?* she wondered. *The next qualifying opportunity won't arrive for four more years. I'll be too old to compete then, and I can't take another year off. I'm doomed.*

But then her inner wisdom spoke up. *Don't give up,* she heard from deep inside. *Train anyway.* Confused, but hopeful, she began to puzzle about the message. *How can I work toward my goal if I can't stand, walk or run? What might I do?*

And then she hatched a plan: She'd use her mind to change her body; she'd train her brain to change her life. She'd tell herself: *I am qualifying for the team* and work to see herself do it. She'd imagine herself in her Olympic outfit and at the games—and she *would* be there!

Carol set to work. She procured tapes of all the prior Olympic races in her category. She watched the winning athletes over and over, slowing the tapes down to analyze their movements frame by frame. Each time she watched a tape, she imagined herself running in the place of that competitor, only faster. She spent hours a day doing this, and she also affirmed herself constantly: *I am outrunning everyone in my category. I am at the Olympics.*

When she was able to stand comfortably on crutches, she stood at the starting line on the track and visualized herself running the course—*fast!* She told herself, *I am winning.* Eventually, she could stand without crutches, and she kept doing the same thing. After some months, she could walk a bit of the track, then a little more, and eventually the whole course. She continued to excel *in her mind,* even though she couldn't really run a single step.

When the qualifying day arrived, Carol had trained daily—in her mind—for a full year, but she hadn't actually run at all. She put on her running clothes, wrapped her ankle and foot in all sorts of protective bandages, and stood at the starting line. The bell rang and she was off, doing what she'd told herself she'd do, enacting what she'd visualized, and living her belief.

And she qualified! She ran her best time ever, and she was going to the Olympics as a member of the U.S. team. She'd talked herself to triumph. Her mind—the things she'd chosen to tell herself over and over, the images she'd called up, and the persistence she'd exhibited—had literally changed her physical being and her destiny.

Can what *you* tell yourself change your mind, body, and life? Of course. You simply have to choose to step into the challenge and do the work persistently and consistently, without fail. Can you visualize and talk yourself to wellness? You certainly can.

What you choose to tell yourself will change your path. Use the daily affirmations you've created, and you *will* take charge of your emotional life.

STEP 7

Learn the Language of Your Body and Make Friends with Your Inner Healer

Welcome to Step 7. So far in your Take-Charge program, you've looked at the possibility that you have a medical condition or clinical disorder, explored your need for medication, learned how to use drugs and complementary and alternative medicine (CAM) for healing, examined the relationship between your nature and life choices, identified the beliefs that imprison you, and begun working at reprogramming your self-destructive brain circuits. You ended Step 6 by reading Carol's story, where you discovered the power of the mind to literally change the body.

In this chapter, you'll examine the ways that your body talks to you—how you physically express your emotional state. You'll learn to use your mind to heed the language of your inner healer, and to register its lessons and make the changes necessary to take charge of your emotional life. You'll do so by traveling back in time to explore your story from another angle, discovering your "body-language fingerprint." You'll then develop affirmations and guidelines to use in accessing and honoring your "body-speak." Finally, you'll learn how to use guided imagery to facilitate your Step 7 work.

EXAMINING PHYSICAL MESSAGES

Often, our body's symptoms are manifestations of our unrecognized psychic pain—of stress, depression, anxiety, grief, and fear. When we're out of touch with our emotional challenges and needs, our bodies feel and express the problem. We may suffer from sleep difficulties, muscle tension, or shortness of breath. We may become irritable, sweaty, short-tempered, tearful, hypertensive, or "wiped out." We can even develop problems such as headaches, colitis, back pain, cardiac disease, asthma, and esophagitis. Sometimes when we're carrying traumas that we don't even realize exist, our bodies struggle to let us know what's going on by making us sick.

Every moment, our physical selves are registering experiences and communicating with us about what's happening. When someone smiles at us, our bodies register joy, our blood pressure and heart rate diminish, and calming chemicals suffuse our systems. We feel good. Yet when another person cuts us off in traffic and gives us the finger, our bodies register upset. Our blood pressure and heart rate rise; we may get sweaty and jumpy. We feel bad.

Scientist and author Candace Pert talks about the molecules of emotion that affect every cell in the body. Hundreds of chemical messengers (informational substances) are registering and communicating emotional experiences throughout our bodies all the time. Whether we recognize it or not, we're physically *feeling* things.

Sometimes our minds can't, don't, or won't register the emotions that impact us. When this disconnect gets large enough, we may feel sick. Our "illness" may take us to the emergency room or to our family doctor. After a thorough assessment and a bunch of tests, we might even be told that there's nothing wrong—in other words, nothing can be found on an exam, x-ray, or blood panel to explain our distress.

But something *is* wrong: We're ill. We feel bad because something is going on, and our bodies are trying to let us know what it is. It's our job to learn the language of our physical selves, to determine what's amiss, and to allow our symptoms to guide us in finding our unique path to wellness. We can all do this, and I'm going to show you how.

Let me give you some examples of what I'm talking about. I'll start by telling you something about how my body talks to me, and how I've learned to heed its lessons.

Developing Awareness: My Story

Many years ago while I was in a residency training program to become a psychiatrist, a psychologist was teaching our class about psychological testing, which is a system of structured questions and exercises designed to be administered and scored to provide help in understanding brain function and diagnoses in patients. He told us that a new computer-based tool had just come out, one that would spit out a psychological profile of anyone who completed a several-page questionnaire. He offered us residents the opportunity to be evaluated in this way so that we could see what we thought of the tool. My whole class chose to do it, and we got our results back the following week.

My profile said that I was a stable, well-adjusted person with an optimistic outlook and a clear sense of self and my goals in life. But it also reported that I had a propensity for somatization—that is, at times I'd feel my distress through physical symptoms such as headaches or stomach pains. *How odd,* I remember thinking. *I have no awareness whatsoever of doing this.* But I hadn't yet learned the language of my body.

The teaching stayed with me, and I began to pay attention to what my body might be telling me that I was missing. I started to appreciate the wisdom in my physical responses to life occurrences. I found that I'd get headaches or stomachaches when I was operating from a place of guilt, or when I was trying to do what I thought I *should,* instead of what I wanted to do.

Each time this occurred, I challenged myself to change my behavior and thus eliminate the symptom. I learned to do it so well that eventually the need for the physical sign went away, and I rarely do anything from a place of "should" or guilt today. On the infrequent occasions that I begin to be drawn in that direction, I start to feel ill or unsettled. At that point, it's my job to stop, look at the situation, listen to myself, and then shift gears.

My body has talked to me in other ways over the years. It has, for example, taught me a lot about how to take charge of my needs in my family life. I've been in a stable, happy marriage with the same man for almost 25 years, but my husband, Rick, and I have been through some challenging times, just as most couples have who stay together long enough.

On several occasions when my husband wasn't dealing with his own issues adequately and his behavior was compromising my well-being and that of our family, I developed weird physical symptoms. There was a period when I had such severe pain in my feet that it hurt to walk or stand. A full medical workup found no abnormality, and I eventually realized that my body was saying, *I can't stand this anymore. I can't keep walking this road. Something has to change or I'll need to leave this relationship.*

On another occasion, I developed severe chest pain that was diagnosed as mild esophagitis. Although the abnormality did show up on an endoscopy, I knew that it was a result of my reaction to my husband's behavior. The pain would come and go, day by day, in response to how comfortable I felt with what Rick was doing to address his problems. My body was saying, *I can't stomach this. I can't take this in. Enough is enough.*

I learned to use these messages from my inner healer to guide me in self-care and marital communication. I spoke and lived my needs. Eventually, my marriage improved and the symptoms resolved.

Our bodies store and remember our histories. Every one of our cells is involved in this process. So, as I sit here writing about these challenging times in my own life, I am actually reexperiencing—in a much milder form—the foot and chest pains I just described. Although my marital problems are long gone, and my husband is on the other side of avoiding challenge, the experiences have become a piece of my personhood. They live in my heart, soul, brain, and body, and your system works the same way. Your body knows, remembers, and has a lot to teach you about how to take charge of your emotional life.

I want to share one more example from my life before I tell you about some patients. This one concerns the language of body memory. When I was in my residency training, I did a rotation under a particularly critical and nasty supervisor. Dr. Jones was the head of a department in the hospital and everyone had to put up with his treatment to get through a required rotation. I found my two months under him to be among the most traumatic of my training years. When they were over, I breathed a deep sigh of relief. Never again would I have to deal with Dr. Jones.

Some years passed, and I graduated and set up my own private practice. Then one day as I was seeing patients in my office, a phone call came in. Between appointments, I checked my voice mail. As soon as I heard Dr. Jones's voice on the recording, I felt anxious. Unsettled, I listened to his brief request that I give him a call. *What did I do wrong?* I found myself thinking. I then immediately reassured myself: *There's nothing he can do to hurt me now.* My body had stored the trauma of dealing with this man, and I had to use my mind to talk back to the fear. But the sensation was also there to warn me: *Stay away from that guy.*

I mustered the necessary courage to call Dr. Jones back. Imagine my surprise when I discovered that he was calling to offer me a job—and my pleasure in being able to politely (and self-protectively) decline the offer!

I want to share a few additional clinical vignettes—examples of different ways our bodies tell us our stories—from my practice. As you read each one, think about your own body's language. How do your cells and organs talk to you?

WORRYING HERSELF SICK: SANDRA'S STORY

I was having coffee with a colleague when she said, "I'm really worried about my friend Sandra. Something is really wrong with her. She has all these neurological symptoms—numbness, weakness, and pain. She had to take a leave of absence from work. She's been hospitalized and evaluated at several medical facilities, but no one can figure out what's wrong with her. Would you be willing to see her?"

Concerned and perplexed, I responded, "Of course."

As I sat with Sandra the next day, she described a significant disconnect between her spiritual life and her work. "I hate my job," she said, "but I don't know what I want to do instead. My spiritual practice is totally separate from everything else I do." As she told me her life story, I kept getting the sense that she wasn't really in the picture. She'd had many interesting experiences, but very few of them seemed to reflect her choices, passions, purpose, or even interests. They sounded more reactive to others than driven by self-knowledge or drive. She was anxious and very self-critical.

Sandra also described her neurological symptoms and the extent of her medical evaluation. She had numbness, weakness, pain, and sensitivity in her arms and legs that would come and go. It didn't follow the usual distribution of any neurological illness. She described the pain as mini-explosions all over her limbs. I thought, *Something is pushing to get out, screaming to be heard.*

As I sat with Sandra and immersed myself in listening to her story, dreams, symptoms, and pains, *my* inner voice began to scream, *There's nothing neurologically wrong with her!* Her workups had been exceptional; it was her *story* that was shouting to be heard. Her body had forced her to pause—to stop doing what she *had* been—so that she could examine and fix her life.

"There's nothing neurologically wrong with you, Sandra," I said, voicing my inner wisdom after sitting with her for two and a half hours. "You're not in your own story. Your body is telling you that you need to stop, take stock, and figure out how to take charge of your life. You need to bring what matters to you together with what you're doing, and I can help you do so. You're going to be fine."

Sandra began to cry with relief; her inner healer had been recognized. "I know you're right," she said. "I'm just so anxious and overwhelmed." Her physical complaints were masking her generalized anxiety. She was scared and confused, not neurologically ill.

"You need to stop focusing on the symptoms," I said. "The more you worry about them, the worse they'll get." I taught her a thought-stopping technique to use whenever she began to worry. You, too, can learn this tool from my *Stop Anxiety Now Kit* (available June 2007 from Hay House), or my first book, *There's Always Help; There's Always Hope.*

I explained that whenever she began to experience the symptoms, she needed to say, "There's nothing wrong with me. I'm just anxious. What is my body trying to tell me?" She could also use some anti-anxiety medicine briefly to take the edge off her worries if she couldn't easily get them to settle down, or if she had trouble pulling herself out of the negative thought loop. The physical manifestations would be quieted, but the real work—the process that would eliminate these signs all together—involved figuring out how to heed the language of her body. We had to determine what she needed to do to take charge of her emotional life.

Recognizing the truth in my explanation, Sandra began to quiet her body with the thought-stopping technique, anxiety management, and self-exploration. She was soon able to return to work and start examining the pieces of her current life that suited her and identify the ones that needed to be changed. Although Sandra isn't finished with her long-term work, she's on the way to wellness, and she's come to see her symptoms as messages from her inner healer. They're to be welcomed, not feared.

Recognizing External Stressors: Frank's Story

Frank, a 53-year-old police officer, was referred to me by a colleague. In his initial phone call, Frank said, "I was abused when I was a kid and treated for depression when I was a young man. I've even been hospitalized for being suicidal. I've been fine for 20 years without therapy or medication, but recently I began to feel that old stuff again. Right now I'm suicidal and overwhelmed. I wonder if you can help me. I just restarted an antidepressant, but I think I need to talk some stuff out." I agreed to see him for evaluation.

When Frank came to see me, he had a great deal of trouble sharing any more of his history. It was clear that he didn't want to talk about his past, or even that much about his current struggles. But he did tell me that a number of his buddies from work had recently been killed in the line of duty, his beat was getting more dangerous, and he was overwhelmed by the amount of trauma and violence that he was exposed to on a daily basis.

"I'm finding it harder and harder to keep my work separate from the rest of my life. I'm hanging on to my job because I have to put in three more years to retire with full benefits and a pension, but it's tough. In the last year, I've developed high blood pressure, depression, severe chest pains, and back troubles. My best friend, a cop who started with me, just had a heart attack. It could easily have been me. I'm in your office now, but I don't really want to talk about my past or my work at all."

"Frank," I said, "your desire not to talk about your history and current trauma is healthy. Your resistance is there for a reason, and we must honor it. You need all your energy to keep on going when you're so overwhelmed. I don't think you can add to your stress by sharing the details of your pain right now. You'd have to relive it in order to do so, and you can't afford to harm yourself that way.

"Your body is screaming to get out of the stress you're under as it is. To keep on working your beat feels so bad to you that you'd rather be dead! How about transferring to another position within the police force for your remaining years? I think your job is killing you. You don't need to do psychotherapy work, because the problem isn't internal. It's between you and what you're trying to force yourself to do. Change your work and I bet that your depression, blood pressure, and back and chest pain will improve. There's a lot of stress-related illness in police officers, firefighters, and other first responders, as well as veterans and other trauma survivors. It's finally catching up with you."

Frank replied, "I know you're right. I just didn't want to admit it to myself, because it's not macho . . . but I have to make a change, and I will. Being a cop takes a big toll on a person. I've put in my time."

He requested a change the next week and was given another job two weeks after that. He and I reconnected after he'd been in his new position for a couple of months. By then, all of his symptoms had resolved: no more high blood pressure, back or chest pain, or suicidal thoughts. He felt well and whole. Having learned to heed the language of his body, he'd healed himself.

Separating the Past from the Present: Lisa's Story

I'd like to share another vignette and affirmation response with you right now. It involves a call I received recently while doing my radio show, *Healing Your Body, Mind, and Spirit.*

Lisa called in and said, "I've been through a lot of trauma in my childhood. I was sexually abused, my house burned down, and I was raped three times. I've gotten a lot of help, but in recent years, I've been more fearful, such as when I'm driving. I often have numbness and tingling. My sleep is terrible and I'm really jumpy."

I told Lisa that she was describing symptoms of post-traumatic stress disorder, which often arise in response to life-threatening experiences (see Step 1). That made sense to her, but she was confused because she'd been better for some years. She wondered why she'd gotten worse since her attack of acute appendicitis and emergency surgery several years ago.

When Lisa developed appendicitis, she had to have an operation immediately in order to save her life. She had no time to think about her situation, and she lost all sense of control. She was told by "powerful doctors" that they'd be putting her to sleep to cut her open and remove her appendix before it burst.

Lisa's experience of helplessness and violation in the emergency room reactivated her physical memory of rape and abuse. As her body began to relive its past, all her associated symptoms came alive, too. Not realizing the trigger, she'd been unable to settle her system again.

While still on the air, I taught her to affirm herself to promote healing. "Lisa," I said, "your surgery led you to relive the trauma of your past. In the hospital, you felt the way you did when you were being abused, but you weren't really in danger. You need to talk to your body, and comfort yourself by saying, *I am in no danger now. The surgery saved my life. My body is remembering old trauma. I am safe now, and I need not fear.*

Relieved and grateful, Lisa thanked me for my time and the guidance. She hung up, empowered. She'd discovered the reason for the return of her symptoms and learned how to affirm her self and quell her worries.

LEARNING YOUR OWN LANGUAGE

Having read my own story, plus Sandra's, Frank's, and Lisa's, you've learned a great deal about how the body identifies emotion and does its job to communicate its wisdom. You've also discovered what it means to register and heed the lessons of an inner healer.

What do you know about the language of *your* body? How do your cells, organs, limbs, and other body parts talk to you? What do they say? How do you express fear, sadness, anxiety, and joy? What happens minute to minute versus long term? How might you register and respond to your body's language? What is it trying to tell you? To whom—me, Sandra, Frank, or Lisa—do you most relate? Do you see bits of your story in all the examples? Please record your thoughts below or on a separate piece of paper:

_____

_____

_____

Your patterns of body-speak are enduring and unique to you. They have early origins and are, in effect, your "body-language fingerprint." Just as your real fingerprint defines you and only you in an ongoing way, so does your physical way of registering, processing, and communicating your experiences.

TIME TRAVEL: WHAT IS MY BODY-LANGUAGE FINGERPRINT?

In an effort to get more in touch with the language of your body, I suggest that you begin thinking about your early years. Call up scenes from your past—moments of joy, challenge, and fear. Visit your earliest memories, perhaps the first day of school, meeting a best friend, birthday celebrations, or a bedtime routine. As you step into your past, pay attention to what your body, mind, and spirit register. Notice your heart beating, your sense of anxiety or peacefulness, and how you feel in general.

Recollect moments of physical discomfort, sickness, and physical strength, and focus on your body. What do you notice? What might you need to pay more attention to if you are to hear your inner voice more clearly?

Now travel forward in time. Visit scenes from your young-adult years and more recent occasions. See yourself at work, at play, and in relationships. Listen in on your conversations; and see and hear yourself speaking, singing, crying, and yelling. Notice your tone of voice, body position, and physical and emotional state. Watch yourself when you feel good and when you feel bad, when you feel safe and when you feel scared. What do you discover?

Think about times in your life when you knew something for sure. How did you feel? Remember times when you silenced your deep knowing. What happened in your body? How did it try to talk to you? How did you respond? What did you learn? Write some of your reflections below or on another piece of paper:

_____

_____

_____

_____

_____

To get more in touch with the language and lessons of your physical self, complete the statements in this exercise without thinking too much. Just focus on your body, and write whatever comes to mind.

My Body Talks

1. When I'm happy, my body_____

2. When I'm sad, my body _____

3. When I'm overwhelmed, I _____

4. When I'm scared, _____

5. I know I'm excited when _____

6. Feeling good _____

7. Stress _____

8. Sickness _____

9. When I feel safe, I _____

10. I make myself sick _____

11. My greatest fear about my health _____

_____

12. Muscle tension _____

13. My heart beats really fast _____

14. Love _____

15. Pain _____

16. My doctor _____

17. Medication _____

18. Body language means _____

19. My inner wisdom _____

20. My job _____

21. Prayer _____

22. Music _____

23. Friends _____

24. My spouse, lover, or best friend _____

25. Cancer _____

26. Heart disease _____

27. Depression _____

28. Anxiety _____

29. Meditation _____

30. Being in nature _____

31. Internal peace _____

32. I self-soothe when _____

33. I heal myself when _____

34. Others help me _____

35. My pet(s)_____

36. Plants _____

37. Balance for me means _____

38. I take charge of my emotional life when _____

_____

39. I listen to the language of my body when _____

_____

40. I honor the wisdom of my inner healer ____ _____

_____

41. I know for sure _____

42. My body always _____

43. I can heal _____

44. I know that out of mind isn't out of body because _____

_____

Now read the 44 statements you've just created. Do you see any patterns? Does anything jump out at you? Are there lessons that you might want to explore or even implement? Perhaps the following example will help clarify that question.

Healing Lessons from the Past: John's Story

When John, a thin and fit 48-year-old gentleman with colitis did the "Time-Travel" and "My-Body-Talks" exercises, he recalled being fat as a child. He saw himself being teased by his peers, recoiling as they called him "Porker" and "Fatso." He then revisited scenes of himself being too sick to go to school, doubled over in pain because his stomach was killing him.

John had never realized that there might be a connection between his abdominal pain and his emotional distress. But as he stepped back into his history, he felt the deep sadness and shame of this period in his life. He discovered that his childhood affliction was a manifestation of his deep psychic distress: It was easier to be sick than to go to school and face the hurt he felt there.

Could this be a pattern? John had come to see me because his bipolar wife, Wendy, was becoming increasingly critical and emotionally attacking of him during her manic episodes. Fearful of setting her off more, he'd been retreating from the relationship. As he did so, his colitis had flared up. He was in a lot of physical pain and couldn't do his daily routine. In his words, he was "a mess."

"I think my body is telling me how upset I am," John said. "The more I avoid confronting Wendy, the worse my stomach gets. I can't go on like this. It's killing me! I need to let her know what's going on. I think she needs to have her medication adjusted again."

Empowered in a new way to take charge of his emotional and physical life, John went on a psychiatric visit with his wife. While there, he described what was happening to him when she was in an altered state. Concerned and deeply distressed to discover what she was doing, Wendy worked productively with her psychiatrist to improve her medication. As her condition improved, John's abdominal pain disappeared.

Begin Identifying Your Body-Speak

Your body is talking to you every single second, and you can become expert at identifying and making sense of its messages. Do you doubt that? Reflect on John's story. Visiting his history, looking for patterns, and acting on the lessons he learned enabled him to heal his marriage and himself. Think about me, and how I became aware of my physical language from a screening tool used in my residency. It taught me to look for my body's expressiveness. As I began to look inward, I discovered emotions that I'd been unaware of before. Paying attention to your body-speak is all it takes to become fluent. And you can learn the language of your system.

Have you ever gotten a cold or virus when you pushed yourself too hard, a headache when you were really anxious, or a stomachache while eating a meal with someone you didn't especially like? Have you ever ended up sick when you just needed a day off or hurt yourself when you couldn't say no in another way? Have you been so exhausted that you couldn't stay awake when you were actually depressed or overwhelmed? Perhaps you've been unable to fall asleep at bedtime because you were deeply troubled by something. Do you remember losing your wallet, locking yourself out of your car, or forgetting your own phone number because you were emotionally overwhelmed? How has your body rebelled when you've pushed yourself beyond what's comfortable for you?

Now think about a time when you felt at peace, calm, or optimistic. Where were you, and what was going on? How has your body rewarded you when you've taken good care of yourself? Write your responses on the lines below or on a separate piece of paper.

_____

_____

_____

By immersing yourself in the language of your body, you might benefit from thinking about your ideas regarding ailments and where they come from. I, for example, was taught by my mom's words and example that physical sickness was acceptable and unavoidable, but emotional distress and psychiatric illness was to be denied and hidden from both the self and others. I routinely heard: "Laugh and the world laughs with you. Cry and you cry alone." Although I now know that lesson is hogwash, it took me years to reprogram it. It's no wonder that I learned to express my distress somatically!

Look at your family history. What illnesses did your mom, dad, siblings, and other relatives have? What was said about these health challenges? What health problems do you have? How do you think and talk about them? Do you see any connection? What did you learn from your parents about sickness, emotional distress, depression, and anxiety? How are those ideas active in your life today? What might you need to do to reprogram your beliefs?

_____

_____

_____

Use the lessons and tools of Step 6 to reprogram the problematic ideas that you identify here by creating the necessary affirmations. For example, to combat the message my mom conveyed, I used something like this: *My healing is about listening, honoring, and sharing my distress. Connection is the route to recovery!*

To combat his fear of conflict, John learned to remind himself, *If my stomach hurts, it probably means that I have to ask for what I need.* And this statement will help combat the fear of somatic symptoms: *When my body talks to me, I listen, learn, and heal.* Write down some affirmations that will help you honor the language of your body:

1. _____

2. _____

3. _____

Write your statements on index cards and say them the way you learned to use affirmations in Step 6. Doing this exercise will help you be open to learning the language of your body and making friends with your inner healer.

You probably realize that Step 7—learning the language of your body and implementing its lessons—actually involves the two smaller steps of discovery and application. This process is similar to the one that you just worked with in the last chapter, where you identified the beliefs that imprison you and reprogrammed the brain circuits involved. Both Steps 6 and 7 require you to figure something out and then actively adjust your behavior as a result of your newfound under-standing; this will be easier to do if you devote some thought to this idea.

As you work Step 7, you should wind up with a series of two-part sentences. Their structure should look something like this:

When my body _____ *, I* _____

Here are some examples of that process as expressed for me, Sandra, Frank, John, and Lisa.

- **Me:** *When* my feet hurt, my body is telling me that I can't go on like this, and *I* need to change the situation or get out. *When* I get anxious upon hearing someone's voice, *I* need to reassure myself of my safety and beware of stepping into an unsafe situation.

- **Sandra:** *When* I feel weird neurological symptoms, my body is telling me that I'm unhappy and anxious in what I'm doing. *I* must stop focusing on my symptoms, calm my anxiety, and change what doesn't work in my professional life.

- **Frank:** *When* I have chest or back pain, high blood pressure, or suicidal thoughts, my body is telling me that I'm trying to do something I can't handle. *I* need to stop right away.

- **John:** *When* my stomach hurts, my body is telling me that I feel criticized and ashamed. *I* need to set limits with the person who's hurting me.

- **Lisa:** *When* my PTSD symptoms arise, my body is revisiting past trauma. *I* need to ensure my current safety, and then reassure myself that I am not at risk.

Take some time to write your two-part statements here or on a separate piece of paper. Remember to use the structure:

When my body _____ *, I* _____

_____

_____

You might want to create additional affirmation statements from these Step 7 Take-Charge sentences. Use the familiar procedure from Step 6 to do so.

PSYCHOTHERAPY AND BODY-SPEAK

Let's talk a bit about the role that psychotherapy might play in helping you master Step 7 of your Take-Charge program. I'd like you to think about the stories I shared in this chapter (mine, Sandra's, Frank's, Lisa's, and John's). Perhaps you realize that therapeutic guidance and support was helpful in each Take-Charge journey.

Does that mean psychotherapy or counseling are always necessary? Absolutely not! But I want you to know that we can all get a little stuck in the mind-body disconnect of this step without someone to offer another perspective. As you work this step, I encourage you to be open to getting outside consultation. Don't hesitate to give voice to your struggles in the company of someone you trust. You may be amazed to discover how much you benefit from a wise advisor.

Remember Sandra, Frank, and John? All found great relief after just a few hours of consultation. They knew that their bodies were trying to tell them a specific truth. But they needed external validation and support to accept and act on what they already knew. Do you feel a resonance with this need? If so, pursue it!

I'd like to close this chapter with a guided-imagery exercise to support you in learning the language of your body and making friends with your inner healer. Our greatest healing happens from a place of peace, presence, self-respect, solitude, and deep personal connection. While in that state, we can access our pain and inner wisdom. We must go there to hear the still, small voice within and be guided toward healing . . . and I'll help you travel to that space.

Practice this technique when you have at least 20 minutes free, are in a comfortable and safe physical space, won't be interrupted, and can play soothing, gentle background music. Think about where you might do this. The more often you complete this exercise, the easier it will be to enter that calm, knowing place.

When you've chosen your space and have the time, dim the lights, get comfortable, turn off all phones and ringers, let others know not to interrupt you, and put on some quiet music if you wish. Make sure that you feel at ease in your space, position, and so on before beginning. When you're ready, read the exercise to yourself, have someone else read it to you, or record it as you read it and then play back your recording. Pause between each sentence and phrase; don't rush the words. Your body will respond to the pace and tone of the language, so be soothing, slow, gentle, and loving to yourself.

GUIDED IMAGERY FOR HONORING YOUR BODY'S LANGUAGE

Take some deep, slow, cleansing breaths. Feel each one as it goes in through your nostrils and out through your mouth; allow your belly to rise and fall. Imagine yourself relaxing into your body more and more each time you breathe.

Feel the floor beneath you—your grounding to Mother Earth. Hear, smell, and feel the wind of your breathing—that miraculous physical manifestation of your being. Notice your body and sense the air around you. You're safe, grounded, and protected by a cushion of healing energy. You're surrounded by warmth, light, love, and gentleness. You're connected to all that heals. Your inner wisdom is brilliant, and you're at peace.

Rest in the knowledge of your safety, the energy of your wholeness, and your place of deep peace. As you breathe into the experience, pay attention to your body's language. Gently notice your arms, legs, head, heart, back, neck, and gut. Allow your roving attention to see, hear, feel, and touch all parts of your being.

Notice, without judgment, what is there. You may feel pain, joy, sadness, heaviness, lightness, burning, or numbness . . . or you may feel other things. Let them all be. Simply observe what is, since all exists for a reason. You're curious, open, and willing to learn. Allow the lessons of your body to come to you.

You may visit all parts of yourself or feel powerfully drawn to certain places. Go where you're called, and explore. Look, listen, sense, feel, and hear . . . and let it be. Notice, observe, experience, and pay gentle attention. Stay in this peaceful attentiveness for as long as you wish, simply noticing what is, welcoming without judgment, being at one and at peace with your body and deep wisdom.

Whenever you're ready, begin to ask your body, your inner healer, yourself: What do you want to teach me? Do you have something to say? Let come what may. Perhaps a powerful lesson, a clue, or nothing will emerge just yet. Whatever happens is meant to be, so just sit in openness. Your inner guidance will emerge when it's time. Don't rush or push; simply be. You'll be given exactly what you need at precisely the right moment. Let your body talk to you, and allow your wisdom to emerge as it's ready. You'll be enlightened . . . you will heal.

Now think of a special destination you'd like to visit. Allow yourself to travel to that wonderful place. Imagine yourself there. Feel, see, hear, and touch your surroundings—perhaps the wind or sun on your cheeks, the grass between your toes, the smell of flowers, or the feel of a recent rain. Know that you can return to this place at any time. Relax gently into this spot and remain there as long as you wish.

When you're ready, emerge slowly from your journey. Savor the peacefulness and wisdom of your trip, carrying it with you as you go forward. Make note of any lessons you've learned. Know that you can return to your healing place at any time . . . and so you will.

We've come to the end of Step 7, and you've learned a lot about the mind-body connection. You've begun to identify the way your body talks to you and figure out how to implement its lessons. You've created some affirmations and guidelines to help you work this step, considered whether a psychotherapy consultation could benefit you, and learned how to use a guided-imagery tool to facilitate your Step 7 Take-Charge efforts.

This work is ongoing, because your body will be talking to you forever. As you continue to use the techniques of this step, you'll become increasingly fluent in the language of your body and adept at using its voice in your healing. Like Sandra, Frank, John, and Lisa, you can master this process, and I know you will!

STEP 8

Share Stories and Build Connections

We need one another. Even the Bible, an ancient record of human history, tells us that when God created Adam, he determined that it wasn't good for man to be alone. So he created a life partner for Adam, and woman was "born." As in the biblical tale, we need one another to face and solve life's problems, care for each other, and ensure the survival of our species.

Whether you believe that the Bible is divinely inspired or not, this lesson is enduring. Connection fosters health, fulfillment, and well-being; while loneliness, isolation, and lack of social support lead to illness and suffering. I often say, "Isolation fuels depression. Disconnection promotes anxiety. Despair destroys lives. Love heals."

We humans are profoundly relational. Our brains, bodies, and spirits are wired to put ourselves in each other's shoes and feel for one another; we want to reach out and help those less fortunate. We also ache to be seen, heard, touched, and understood. We want our stories to be known, to have someone care about what happens in our day, and to matter to our friends and neighbors. We're happiest when we're in fulfilling relationships. We thrive when we know that others are there for us—that someone will drive us to the doctor when we're too ill to take ourselves, lend us money if we come upon tough times, and remember our birthdays.

We've evolved in communities for a good reason. Many studies have shown the importance of love and connection to wellness and longevity. When you feel cared for, nurtured, and supported, you're more likely to be happy and healthy than when you feel lonely and isolated. Furthermore, when you get sick, you have a much greater chance of getting better if you aren't on your own. Dr. Dean Ornish has compiled a lot of studies that show the relationship between connection and well-being in his book *Love & Survival* (which I mentioned earlier). He demonstrates that loneliness and isolation increase the likelihood of disease and premature death from all causes by 200 to 500 percent or more! We really do need one another.

Unfortunately, when it comes to respect for this enduring wisdom, we're living in particularly scary and challenging times. Recent advances in technology, globalization, and economic forces that keep us at work for most of our waking hours have conspired to destroy much of what has kept us connected and healthy for countless generations. Too many of us are living on the edge of despair, disconnection, and burnout. As a result of our isolation and time-challenged lives, we're experiencing more depression, anxiety, distress, disease, and addiction. More and more college students have serious mental-health issues each year, and baby boomers face a growing incidence of clinical depression. We're in a lot of trouble as a society, and it isn't getting better.

Think about it: How many people really know your story? How many of those are paid by you in some way (such as your masseuse, housekeeper, hairdresser, or therapist)? How much time do you spend hanging out—without every minute scheduled—with people you care about? Do you routinely drop in to see your neighbors? Do friends often call you to talk? If so, do you have time to visit with them when they do? How often do you do two things at once, such as drive and talk on the phone, or check your messages while you're in line at the supermarket?

How many nights a week do you eat a family (or household) meal at home? Do you take the time to cook or prepare your food? When is the last time you borrowed an egg or a cup of sugar from a neighbor? How much television do you watch? What games do you play on the computer, when you could be visiting with another person instead? How often do you e-mail someone because it's easier than finding the time to talk? And how many times do you leave voice-mail messages or play "phone tag" without actually connecting with the other party?

How much of your life do you actually share with your best friend or life partner (if you have one)? If you're a parent, how often do you visit with your child or children without distractions—just sharing stories, ideas, concerns, and observations? What would you rather do: read a book or see a movie? How much of a real "neighborhood" do you live in—in other words, are there kids on the street playing ball or riding bikes in good weather? Do you take walks around the block and know most of the people you pass along the way? Where do you feel a sense of belonging in your life?

How long have you lived in the same town, county, state, or even country? How many long-term relationships do you have? How often do you choose FedEx over "snail mail," e-mail over a phone call, or fast food over a home-cooked meal?

How many people are "there" for you? Who would you call to take you to the emergency room, lend you money, or sit with you if a loved one were in surgery? How many folks would step in to support you if your home burned down or you got sick? How many would help you out in times of need? How much do you give back, sharing of your time, energy, and gifts? Would others notice if you went away for some weeks without telling them that you'd be gone? Who would call to check in on you? How many people know your routines? Do you know anyone else's habits? More than one person? How many?

If you're like most people, you're working more hours than your parents had to for a comparable lifestyle. You have less leisure time, are more stressed, feel routinely anxious and behind on your responsibilities, and see no end to the challenge. You go on vacation to relax but get overwhelmed with what you need to do in order to get away. You then come home to more pressure than you left originally. Upon returning, you may even question the value of leaving in the first place!

Like many others, you probably grew up in a more connected world than you now inhabit. You spent more time playing with friends without needing the structure and entertainment that characterizes kids' playdates today. You often made last-minute plans to eat dinner with a friend, comparing menus and deciding which one was more appealing. You could do that because everyone ate at home at about the same time. Very few families do that anymore; and most kids have too much homework, participate in a bunch of extracurricular activities, and are running just as hard as their folks.

If you're like many, you have very few real intimate and enduring relationships and can count on one hand the number of people that you rely on to be there in a crisis. You may feel lonely, isolated, and disconnected more often than you'd like to admit.

You see, I know what goes on in the intimacy of people's lives, because I hear about it all the time. Almost everyone is feeling this pain of disconnection. And I know from my own personal life as a wife, mom, doctor, and teacher how lonely it can be to live in our "advanced" society. We're too busy to be there for ourselves and for one another.

To be connected to others, we must first be in touch with ourselves, and as you know from Step 7, our inner connection can only come if we make space for solitude. But we don't seem to be good at doing that. We're bombarded with stimulation, and we're always running because we can't seem to get caught up. But this frenetic life we lead is a real crisis, a disaster, and even a potential death sentence. We crave connection; we need one another.

I've learned, both from my own life experiences and from having the opportunity to hear about the lives of many brave souls, that no matter how hard it is, we need to stop running. We've got to take time to be with ourselves and listen to our thoughts, bodies, and inner wisdom. We've got to shut out the distractions, silence the background noise, and force ourselves to create and protect be-with-myself time. We must recharge.

And then, from our place of greater wholeness, we've got to *work* at building connections into our lives. We have to swim against the current, making sure that what has healed us as a people from one generation to the next doesn't get lost in the race to advance. This isn't easy to do. The concept is simple, but it takes a big effort to implement . . . and doing so is crucial to our survival.

See, we all know deep down that we'll never get everything done and that there's always more to do. We know that we can fill every moment of our lives trying to succeed and wind up on our death beds wondering what we did with our precious time here on Earth. When most people are asked what they want to be remembered for, what matters most to them in life, or how they'd spend their remaining days if they only had a few left, the majority focus on relationship issues. They want to matter to someone, to love and be loved, and to contribute to making someone's life better.

We most value oneness, love, and connection, yet we don't make these things enough of a priority in our lives. As a result, we're unhappy and unwell. We're making ourselves sick, and we've got to stop it. We have to change our focus and build connections. We can take charge of our love lives, and we can heal.

In this step, you'll consider the degree of connection and isolation you experience in your life. How often do you share your story or really listen to others? You'll learn communication skills to foster intimacy. And after studying a list of ten tools that you can use to build your Step 8 Take-Charge strategy, you'll choose to implement the ones best suited to your needs.

In answering the questions I posed earlier in this chapter, you've already begun examining your life for connections and disconnects. As you move into deeper self-reflection, I'd like to talk to you about the healing power of sharing our stories. What happens when we do that? Why is it so beneficial?

WHY SHARE STORIES?

We need to talk to others so that when we lose touch with ourselves, they can remind us of who we are and what we've lived. In sharing our tales, we can gain perspective; balance out our negativity; be accepted when we have trouble approving of ourselves; and clarify our own thoughts, feelings, and ideas. We each exist in relationship to others. As we listen and respond to one another, we come to know and understand ourselves a little better. Let's look at some examples of these benefits of sharing our stories. (Although there's overlap among all these concepts and examples, we're examining each of them individually so that you get a good sense of why you need to share your story in order to take charge of your emotional life.)

Others Remind Us of Who We Are and What We've Lived

I see this first benefit active in my work all the time. Often, patients will come in overwhelmed, down on themselves; or hopeless about their ability to change, grow, or make progress. But having worked with them for some time and seen dramatic change take place already, I can say something such as: "Remember when you first came to see me—depressed, unemployed, and on the verge of divorce? You've climbed out of that hole, found a new job, and turned your life around. Your marriage is on the mend, and you often see light at the end of the tunnel. Perhaps you're having a bad week, but you're nowhere near the dark place you started from."

Here's another example of how sharing our stories enables others to remind us of our own tales. This one is about my son Gabriel (again!). He recently came home from basketball practice upset and said, "I played great. I've been doing really well all week, and I'm not getting recognition!"

"Gabe," I said with a smile, "you're doing *great?* And you're upset *not to be recognized?* I thought you were going to tell me that you played badly. It wasn't that long ago that you considered dropping the sport because you weren't good enough. What's this about?"

In a split second, Gabe's mood and facial expression changed. With a big smile on his face, he said, "You're right, Mom! What's important is my improvement. It's about the sport." And off he went to get a snack from the kitchen—full of joy in his progress.

Here's a third example. To be fair, I'll share an anecdote about my older son, Benjamin—a high school senior who's applying to colleges right now. A lot of the essay questions he must complete require him to describe his goals, passions, career plans, and accomplishments. But, like most 17-year-olds, Ben hasn't thought about his story in that way.

He's known for a long time that he wants to be a pediatrician and that he's great with kids and adults of all ages. But before our family caucuses about filling out college applications, he didn't even remember all the places where he'd worked that involved teaching and caring for kids. Once we reviewed his work history with him, he recognized how his passion had been manifesting for years. In coming to know himself better through our feedback, he figured out what to write on his applications.

⁓

Think about the power of having others know you well enough to be able to remind you of your own story when you most need to hear it. When have you had experiences like that in your life? Could you benefit from more? Record your thoughts here or on a separate piece of paper:

_____

_____

_____

Sharing Our Stories to Gain Perspective

The first illustration of this powerful benefit is from my own life. I'll never forget one especially painful time when I was feeling a lot of financial pressure to provide for my family and my marriage was in its rocky phase. I planned to do a day-long seminar on whole-person healing—out of my own desperation, I think. The program was to include a large workbook and many other materials. Brochures went out, and people began to register.

But I was in no place to create all the needed materials by the seminar date. Since I'd said I would do so, I began to feel like a failure. This was one of the only times in my life when I'd committed to something and then felt unable to follow through. I did realize my error several months in advance, in plenty of time to refund registration fees and cut my losses, but I'd let myself down and couldn't stop beating myself up.

Finally, I shared my self-critical perspective with my husband, who was loving and humorous. "You never do things like this," he said. "You always do whatever you say you're going to—you're amazing that way. But you're only human. This mistake you made, I make regularly. I often have trouble meeting deadlines and balancing my time. Give yourself a break. It's no big deal."

Upon hearing Rick's words, I was able to regain perspective. What he said was completely correct and totally true. I needed to learn my lesson and let go of my self-flagellation. It *was* "no big deal."

In my clinical practice, I often help my patients by offering perspective. We all need this when we're anxious, overwhelmed, or depressed. When overwrought, we see things in ways that are out of whack and need reality checks to get back on track. Remember Sam's story in Step 6? He was convinced that his job was in jeopardy when his boss hadn't responded to his messages, but he later learned that his boss had the flu. His therapy session involved helping him regain perspective.

How often do you get a more realistic view of the situation from sharing your story with others? What comes to mind? Could you benefit from more input?

_____

_____

_____

Balancing Our Negativity by Sharing Ourselves with Others

Perhaps you've read my first book, *There's Always Help; There's Always Hope.* If so, you know the story of Gillie, a woman in her 40s who came to me with dissociative identity disorder, and who's now well. In my many years of work with this patient, I'd routinely hear her say, "I'm bad. I'm ugly. I'm stupid," and many other self-critical things.

Invariably, I responded, "I don't see you that way." I'd go on to tell her how I *did* view her. I believe that hearing my consistent, supportive remarks—my antidotes for her negative judgments—played a big role in enabling Gillie to transform her self-concept and heal.

In my work, I often hear people say, "I can't do that," when they don't really know for sure, or "No one values my opinion," when they haven't even tried to share it. I'm regularly struck by how self-critical we all seem to be—how much we focus on the ways we're fat, unattractive, poor, stupid, friendless, loveless, or just not enough. By sharing our stories, our inner dialogue, with those who care about us, we open ourselves up and come to realize that we're not alone. Many of our friends—the ones we see as "more than" us—feel about themselves the way we do about ourselves. This learning is healing: We're not alone in our pain, and we're not as bad off as we often believe.

Think about the ways in which sharing your stories with others (or hearing theirs) have helped or would help challenge your negativity. Write your thoughts below or on a separate piece of paper.

_____

_____

_____

Others Accept Us When We Have Trouble Approving of Ourselves

Perhaps the *greatest benefit* you'll gain from sharing of yourself in this way is the acceptance you'll feel from others—even when you're unable to accept yourself. I think that this is why all the 12-step recovery-program meetings are set up to encourage personal sharing. And no matter what people say after being called on to speak, they're always thanked for their participation.

In AA it's said, "You're only as sick as your secrets." When you give honest voice to whatever you carry, you'll be received, and you'll heal. They also say, "Just keep coming back." Whoever you are, whatever your journey, just show up and let others in. In doing so, you will recover.

Another example of the deep healing power that comes from acceptance is to be found in the statement "I love you." What a heartwarming, validating, change-the-world experience we have in hearing those words! When we let others in enough to know and love us through thick and thin, we open ourselves to great joy, fulfillment, peace, and self-acceptance. Remember, love heals, and without it, we die.

Think about times you've been accepted and/or loved by others, whether or not you felt worthy. What comes to mind? Who, when, where, and how? Do you make yourself (safely) vulnerable enough to others in order to experience the depth of love and commitment you want to have in your life? If not, what gets in the way? Record your thoughts on the next page or on a separate piece of paper.

_____

_____

_____

TALKING ABOUT OURSELVES CLARIFIES OUR THOUGHTS, FEELINGS, AND IDEAS

My patients frequently apologize to me as they begin telling me about something—for not having thought it through enough, for not really knowing exactly what's bothering them or what they need. But I reassure them: "That's exactly why you're talking about this. You know that something is bugging you—something needs to be figured out—but you're not sure what yet. As you talk and I ask you questions, we'll figure it out together." Often, they'll even realize what they're thinking or feeling *as they hear themselves* speaking!

At other times, patients will describe inner dialogues or share scenarios because they need help in making sense of them. For example, a woman named Karen told me: "I'm feeling restless, and I've been feeling that way for a while. It's coming to me that I want to change almost everything about my routine, my life, where I live, how I go through my day, and who I talk to. But I know that's just a restlessness—it's not edited or clear at all, this desire to start over somewhere else."

I listened to her describe her dream and devalue her inner voice. Knowing her well enough to realize that her "restlessness" made a lot of sense as she pursued her healing journey, I said, "Karen, what you said was beautiful. It was very clear, and it makes a lot of sense to me. You live where you've lived your whole life, yet you have negative associations with many of the people and places around you. Much of your history here has been traumatic. And you're at a point in your healing journey where you can begin to choose where you want to live and what you want to do from a healthy place. Honor the restlessness. It's healthy to do so, because it's there for a reason."

Karen listened carefully to my words and thanked me once I'd finished. Through her tone of voice, she conveyed her sense of relief and powerful validation. I'd helped her realize the meaning of her musings.

On another occasion, my patient Patricia said, "Can I just talk about what happened between me and my mother-in-law? I'm not exactly sure what to say, but we had a big fight. I know I need to learn something about my issues and about how to deal with her differently, but I have no idea how to understand the problem or what I'm doing wrong."

As we visited the history of the relationship and the specifics of the recent fight, it became clear that Patricia was looking to her mother-in-law for love and validation that she wasn't going to get there. Having been abused by her own mother for many years, she was looking for someone to fill this maternal role in the wrong place. Oftentimes, when her husband's mom would behave as in-laws often do and treat her as just a relative by marriage, Pat would feel wounded. She'd get angry and demand things that the woman wasn't prepared to give. Fights would invariably ensue.

As soon as Pat saw this dynamic clearly, she knew what to do to better care for herself and to repair the relationship. The insight that came from sharing her dilemma was powerfully healing.

Think about the ways and times that you've clarified your own thoughts, feelings, and ideas by opening yourself to others. What have you learned? Who has helped you, and in what ways? Do you talk about yourself enough or too much? Do you ask for input and listen to what others have to say? Write your reflections below or on a separate piece of paper.

_____

_____

_____

CULTIVATING INTIMACY: ISSUES IN COMMUNICATION

By now you've devoted a lot of thought to how much connection you experience in your life. You've also explored the ways you share and withhold your story. You understand the importance of cultivating intimacy as you take charge of your emotional life. You probably recognize that you need to push yourself to be more open and trusting with others.

But you may be fearful of making yourself more vulnerable. Or you may be trying to connect but keep finding that you have trouble getting close to others in spite of your attempts to do so. So let's look at fear and communication issues a bit.

It's always scary to share ourselves. In doing so, we make ourselves vulnerable to criticism, rejection, or abandonment. As I discussed in Step 5, we're powerfully driven by the need for approval. As kids, we all need this from our parents in order to survive. The teaching to be what others want or need you to be is deeply ingrained. We can carry the dread of disapproval forward in profound ways. In some deep and primitive fashion, we may fear for our survival when we aren't accepted for who we are.

Additionally, the more we open ourselves to others—the more we share our weak, sensitive, and vulnerable spots—the more likely we are to be hurt. Those who know us best can support us most, but they can also injure us very deeply. They can attack us in ways that wound, and they can abandon us both emotionally and physically. Whenever we step into intimacy, we invariably accept great joy and deep pain. They come together; we can't have one without the other.

But we're not in danger the way we were as kids. As adults, we can weather, survive, and grow stronger each time we're hurt. In fact, from our pain we learn about joy. In losing someone, we learn what we have; when in the valley, we often develop a greater love for the mountain. We need the downs of life to recognize and appreciate the ups. And most people who love or have loved deeply say that the heartache is a small price to pay for the magic, wonder, and deep joy found in the bond with another.

So I urge you to push yourself to be open. Use affirmations, visualizations, psychotherapy, prayer, and whatever else you need to empower yourself to take risks. Open your heart, mind, and soul to other human beings. Don't allow fear to limit, govern, or control you. Step into your life fully, wholly, and optimistically. The universe will support you in your efforts. You need not fear.

But how are you supposed to talk to other people? And what does it really mean to listen? What is healthy, effective communication? These are crucial questions for us to explore. We often think that we're communicating, when we're actually building walls and setting up barriers. We routinely judge, devalue, and criticize one another without even realizing what we're doing. We focus on the other people instead of ourselves, and we usually tell them what they should do or what they're doing wrong. But the kind of sharing that fosters intimacy is accepting, supportive, respectful, humble, and most important, nonjudgmental.

In order to help you communicate more effectively, I want to give you a template to use when talking about yourself and working to connect with others:

Say the following, inserting a statement of fact and a feeling word:

When you _____**[a]**_____, *I feel* _____**[b]**_____.

[a] = a nonjudgmental statement of fact, such as "walk out of the room while I'm speaking"
[b] = a feeling word or a description of an emotional state, such as "hurt" or "devalued"

Be sure not to add the words *like, that,* or *as if* after the word *feel* in the above template. As soon as you do so, you shift the focus away from you and your feelings, onto the other person. You're then likely to say something critical about him or her.

You probably realize that judgments create distance between people. In contrast, when we share our pain, struggles, joys, and challenges with one another, we foster empathy and connection. This honest kind of sharing in which you make yourself vulnerable is healing.

Use the template from this section to increase the degree of connection you experience as you work Step 8 of your Take-Charge program.

TOOLS TO BUILD A CONNECTION

In the final portion of this chapter, you'll consider a series of connection-building tools or strategies. As you read through each of the ten suggestions, think about which ones you'd like to incorporate in your Take-Charge process. At the end of this section, you'll find a place to record your thoughts and commit to your plan on paper. The suggestions you'll explore are:

1. Be present.
2. Listen to learn.
3. Share feelings.
4. Commit to being there.
5. Open yourself to the experiences of others.
6. Reach out and touch someone.
7. Join a group.
8. Plant a garden.
9. Care for a pet.
10. Create partnerships.

1. Be present. So much of the time when we're in the company of others—even when we're talking to them—we aren't really present. We answer our cell phones in the middle of discussions, work on our computers while listening to our spouses, and pay bills while on the phone with our dear friends and relatives. Think about this phenomenon for a moment. Do you feel heard and received by others when they're multitasking as you're trying to share an experience with them? How often are you the one who's not *really* there for someone else?

So often when we could be present for the person next to us in line at the supermarket or the beauty of the sunrise just in front of us, we're really elsewhere. We're on the phone, checking our Blackberries for e-mail, or tuned in to our iPods. We're busy planning or worrying about tomorrow and losing all connection to today. We're strung out, unsettled, and out of touch with whoever and whatever might heal us.

Suggestion: Choose to do one thing at a time for an hour each day, week, or even month. Decide to keep your cell phone off whenever you're visiting with a friend. Or, out of the myriad of internal and external distractions you bring into your own life, pick one to cut down or eliminate all together.

2. Listen to learn. How often do you listen to others just so that you know when it's time for you to talk and share back? And how many times have you spoken of your needs, hurts, or challenges only to feel misunderstood or dismissed by the other person?

Although few of us do this, we need to step into the other person's experience as we visit with one another. Many faith traditions teach the ideas *Treat your neighbor as yourself* or *Do unto others as you would have them do unto you.* We must learn what it's like to be the other. An ancient Native American proverb says: "Do not criticize your neighbor until you have walked a mile in his moccasins." Cultivating empathy should be the goal of communicating. And empathy—love of the other—is what heals.

Suggestion: Look at how often you engage in conversation to learn about the experience of another. Think about someone in your life whose story you barely know, or reflect on a time when you gave advice before fully understanding the challenge that someone was trying to describe. Consider your prejudices, your unchallenged beliefs about those less fortunate or privileged than you.

Decide to get to know someone better, to listen longer in conversation before giving advice, or to expand your mind and consider new ideas about what might lead a group of people to be as they are. Figure out some way to cultivate more empathy for others in your life.

3. Share feelings. Remember the lesson you learned in the "Cultivating Intimacy" section of this chapter? You make the greatest connection to others when you use "I feel . . ." statements in conversation. Becoming proficient in this way of communicating takes practice, and you might even want to pick up a copy of my first book, *There's Always Help; There's Always Hope,* to work on this skill. It contains a Feelings Vocabulary, an extensive list of words that you can use to become adept at naming your emotional state. It's really important to your growth to let others know how you're feeling. Strange as it may seem, the more ashamed, scared, isolated, less than, or alone you feel, the more benefit you'll gain from letting others in. You're never as bad off as you think or feel you are.

Suggestion: Look at how often you let others know what you're feeling. Is this an area of strength for you? How can you improve? Pick one person in your life with whom you'll try to be more open. It could be a friend, relative, or therapist. What do you need to share? Commit to telling them.

4. Commit to being there. One of the most important things you can do to build connection is to resolve to be there for others. This may mean getting married; choosing to become a parent; being someone's best friend or exercise buddy; or joining a committee at your local church, school, or town hall. It might involve signing up to deliver meals to the homeless every Tuesday, walking your friend's dog twice a week, or even participating in the Big Brothers Big Sisters program and helping a needy child.

The most crucial element of this suggestion and what makes it healing is its consistency in your life. You do it on a regular basis. You know you'll be there, and others can count on your presence.

Suggestion: Examine your commitments. Are there enough of them in your life? What do you reliably do? What can people count on you for?

Plan to add an additional responsibility to your life, or adjust your involvement in one of your ongoing roles or activities to reflect your desire for greater connection. Or stop doing something you're already committed to in order to take on something that you can do more regularly or wholeheartedly.

5. Open yourself to the experiences of others. We can build connections by learning about others through magazines, newspapers, lectures, classes, films, and excursions. This is a way to immerse ourselves in another's way of life, day-to-day challenges, and individual triumphs without even knowing that person. We tap into our own potential for pain, pleasure, hope, despair, triumph, and inspiration by visiting the journeys of our fellow travelers. In doing so, we're often moved to make a difference.

Suggestion: Think about how often you step into someone else's experience through mediums other than conversation. Would you benefit from doing more? Consider taking a class, reading a memoir or social commentary, joining a book group, or watching a documentary. Choose one way to increase your knowledge of another person's world.

6. Reach out and touch someone. There are so many ways to connect with one another. We can, of course, do so physically with a handshake, hug, kiss, or even massage. But we can also do it with a smile, a compliment, a willingness to let someone pull in front of us in traffic, a thank-you, a "thinking-of-you" note, a piece of candy, a charitable donation, an invitation, a volunteer job, or a home-cooked meal.

We touch one another when we offer or receive help, support, concern, or acknowledgment. And it takes so little from us to say, "Have a blessed day," "Thank you for thinking of me," or "I'm so glad you're in my life." We don't do this enough. Instead, we often ignore, criticize, and attack one another way more than we reach out and give back. But remember, love is what heals.

Suggestion: Think about how much you do to reach out and touch others. How often do you offer little niceties to those you care about? How about to strangers? How much do you share of what you have?

Choose someone to connect with, and list three things that you'll do to make their week just a little more pleasant. Decide to say "Thank you" whenever someone extends themselves to you, or to engage in a few random acts of kindness every Sunday. Pick anything else you want to do to reach out and touch someone, and then make sure you do it!

7. Join a group. Whenever people come together around shared interests, values, or needs, miracles happen. The immediate connection that results from sharing a challenge or purpose is deeply healing. I've seen wonderful things occur when people join regular yoga or exercise classes, meditation groups, churches, synagogues, ashrams, book clubs, or supportive gatherings (such as AA, OA, Weight Watchers, and bereavement groups). In fact, I could make a list of possible organizations for you to join that would fill an entire book! The number of psychotherapy and support groups alone is huge.

Suggestion: Think about the groups you belong to. How many are there? What's the purpose of each one? Do they fit your values and needs? Are you a regular participant? Would you do well to join an additional community or to increase your level of involvement in one you belong to already? Make a list of those that appeal to you, and compare it with a rundown of your current activities. Then bring the two lists into alignment. Commit to increasing your involvement in things that matter to you, because you'll build connections this way.

8. Plant a garden. Life is about planting seeds. Much of what we do is like planting a garden—digging holes; putting possibilities into the ground; nurturing what might grow with sun, water, fertilizer, and love; and waiting to see what emerges from our efforts. The bulk of what happens is unseen and silent, under the ground. But then, wonder of wonders, a tender shoot pokes through the earth, and before we know it, we're looking at a marigold, a daisy, or a morning glory.

Taking charge of your emotional life is like planting a garden. You're doing things moment by moment that have no obvious impact at the time; sometimes they may even seem useless or crazy. But then, like the shoot that pokes up through the earth, they begin to pay off. You start to see dramatic change, transformation, and real healing in yourself.

Given these similarities, it probably won't surprise you to learn that caring for plants is deeply healing. Having and maintaining a relationship with the wonder of trees and flowers—living things that depend on you and enrich your life in return—fosters a sense of meaning, peace, and deep connection to the mystery of existence. Many spiritual journeys inward occur in nature, whether beneath a tree, beside a river, or on a mountaintop. Connection to the natural world is deeply beneficial for personal growth . . . and it might just start with pulling weeds.

Suggestion: Think about your connection to plants, trees, flowers, and nature in general. Do you spend enough time outdoors, tending to plants, or arranging flowers? Do you even take the time to smell a rose or walk barefoot upon freshly cut grass? When is the last time you collected beautiful fall leaves or visited an arboretum?

Plan to spend some time in nature each week. Decide if this means tending to a houseplant, weeding a garden, or taking a walk beneath the tall oak trees in your neighborhood. Figure out what it means to you to plant a garden, and start doing so.

9. Care for a pet. How many times have you smiled upon seeing a cute puppy, a tiny kitten, or a foal struggling to stand for the first time? Do you feel better after petting a bunny or cuddling an affectionate dog? Would you rather buy a calendar with scenes of baby animals or still-life paintings on each page? What feelings come up when you remember a beloved animal from your childhood?

Pets heal. Our ongoing relationships with these creatures augment our immune function, increase our experiences of meaningfulness, and lengthen our days. We live longer if we have these companions in our lives.

Suggestion: Think about your involvement with animals. Do you have pets? Have you had them in the past? Do you volunteer at a local animal shelter or feed the ducks at your local pond? In what ways does being with these creatures heal you? Is it through viewing pictures, petting them, observing them, joining the Sierra Club, or caring for them yourself? How might you bring a relationship with animals into your life? Pick some action that makes sense to you and begin doing it. You'll probably be surprised to discover how healing this activity can be.

10. Create partnerships. You've probably heard these expressions:

- The whole is greater than the sum of its parts.

- One plus one equals more than two.

- What we create together is more wonderful than what either one of us could come up with alone.

These statements all speak to the notion that there's greater potential between "us" than there is within each person alone. Remember what you read at the beginning of this chapter, that ancient biblical message: *It is not good for man to be alone. We need one another.*

How many people do you partner with in life? Consider your spouse, lovers, aunts, uncles, cousins, siblings, children, friends, colleagues, therapists, personal trainers, mind-body healers, doctors, lawyers, coaches, accountants, committee members, fellow church members, and whoever else comes to mind. Think about the nature and quality of each relationship. Which ones enhance your life? Are there enough of them?

Suggestion: After taking a careful inventory of the number and quality of your partnering relationships, reflect on how well you build connections that change an "I-you" dynamic into a "we." With whom on your list can you reasonably say one plus one is greater than two? Can you say that often enough?

Decide to increase the number or quality of your partnerships. Do so by hiring a coach, revisiting the rules of engagement with a friend, or cultivating relationships with co-workers who are like-minded. Do whatever works for you to build productive connections in your life. You need to partner, and you can do so to great personal advantage.

You've come to the end of Step 8, so take some time to reflect on what you've learned. How have you benefited from sharing your story with others? Where do you get hung up? What are you planning to change? Which connection-building strategies do you intend to implement as part of your Take-Charge program? Record your insights and plan below, or on a separate piece of paper.

_____

_____

_____

I want to congratulate you on how far you've come. You've now visited and worked eight steps and have acquired many more tools! You deserve hearty acknowledgment: Bravo to you! I encourage you to say these words to yourself: *Bravo to me!*

Celebrate your successes to date, and allow the pleasure you generate by doing so to spur you on in your healing journey. You *can* take charge of your emotional life, and you are *well* on your way to doing so!

STEP 9

Live in the Power of the Possible

Welcome to Step 9: Live In the Power of the Possible. We live in seemingly impossible and challenging times. We're bombarded with negativity and a focus on what doesn't work, on all that's wrong. Most of our "breaking news" is about death, danger, disease, violence, and corruption. As we watch TV, listen to radio news broadcasts, read the headlines on our computer screens, and peruse our local newspapers, we're absorbing a lot of negative energy. We're struck by what a miserable world we inhabit, and we may even find ourselves feeling depressed, anxious, overwhelmed, or numb. We can only take so much of this, but it may seem as if we're surrounded by blackness. We hear so few stories about the power of human potential, the ability of humankind to triumph over adversity, or the benefits that come from doing good deeds.

Whether we recognize it or not, messages such as "The world is dangerous," "Bad things constantly happen to good people," and "You never know who you can trust" begin to seep in. Our anxiety, self-doubt, and potential for despair are activated by the media. Beyond that, marketing messages that encourage us to focus on our faults, problems, and limitations (in order to sell us the solutions) further feed our experiences of personal failure, impossibility, and hopelessness. We may think, *I'm not enough, and I never will be. Why bother?*

I'm deeply troubled by how often we're told to "be realistic," that achieving our hopes and dreams is impossible, and that we need to accept our lot in life and defer to those who "know better." I worry about how little we're encouraged to trust our guts; to believe in the power of what's possible; and to search for guides, mentors, doctors, and supporters who can help us actualize our gifts. I wish that I'd been given a flowering plant each time a person told me that my first book wouldn't sell or that I'd never find a "partner" in a publishing house. I'd have a beautiful garden by now!

So much of the anxiety, distress, and depression that we all experience is a result of how much we live in the power of *impossibility*. We've learned to tell ourselves: *I'm not good enough, I can't do that, There's no use in trying, They're out to get me,* and *The little guy can't succeed against the behemoth corporation.* We've learned to feel helpless. Progressively more victimized by the messages that surround us, we're prone to despair, checking out, and giving up.

But we *can* overcome! I have unflagging faith in the power of the human spirit to triumph over adversity. I believe in you and your capacity to create miracles. I know that by learning to live in the Power of the Possible, you can transform your life. You can find options where there were none, joy where there was only pain, and fulfillment where there was just despair. In Step 9, I intend to teach you how to do that.

But what does it mean to live in the Power of the Possible? What must you tell yourself day in, day out? How can you neutralize and transform the forces of negativity within your mind and in the world around you?

Do you remember *The Little Engine That Could?* If not, go out and get yourself a copy of this wonderful children's book, and read it over and over. It's the story of how a poor, tired little blue engine who'd never made it over the big hill before was willing to take a chance and try to help out another train whose engine had broken down. The broken train was carrying toys for all the children on the other side of the mountain. Many more powerful engines had already come by and refused to help; they were full of excuses.

But the little blue engine was willing to step into the power of possibility. Wanting to help, she was committed to trying to accomplish what would be a huge feat for her. She chose to attempt what many would say was impossible, and she was successful!

So how did she do it? First, she was willing to say yes. And then, mustering every single bit of energy she had, she began pushing herself and pulling all of the cars full of toys behind her. As she slowly but surely began to climb the hill, she kept affirming herself, *I think I can—I think I can—I think I can.* And believing in the possibility that she could triumph, she did.

You see, she didn't know for sure. So she didn't say, "I will succeed," but she surely didn't know that she couldn't either. Unlike many of the more able and powerful engines who said, "I can't," she chose to open herself to the possibility that she could. She was willing to believe in what might be, to act in accordance with it, and thus bring it about. This is what it means to live in the Power of the Possible. You must be willing to believe in the energy of what *might be* and then choose to step fully into doing what must be done to enable that possibility to be actualized.

Living this way means challenging your negativity, false assumptions, and laziness. It involves committing to affirm yourself, push yourself, and surround yourself with those who believe in you. It requires you to monitor yourself for those "impossible" messages, to challenge them whenever they arise, and to remind yourself of what just might be.

Think about it. How often do you say: "I can't," "They won't," "It's hopeless," or "It will never work," when you don't know for sure you're right? And how frequently do you tell yourself (or others): *It's too much effort, It's not worth it,* or *Why bother?* when doing whatever "it" is could yield awesome results? Have you ever been heard to say "That's impossible" when the reality is that it's not, or "It's crazy to think I could do that" when you're just too scared to try? Have you said "I give up" before you put forth your very best effort? Have you ever refused to get help when you were struggling with something because you thought, *If I can't do it myself, it can't be done?* How many times have you given up on a relationship that mattered to you—be it with a friend, co-worker, or relative—without even talking about the problem because it was "too difficult" or "it just couldn't be worked out"?

Record your thoughts below or on a separate piece of paper.

If you're like most of us, you've done all of the above many times. We all get stuck in "impossible" thinking some times, and we're never well served when we do.

I'd like to tell you a story about the power of possibility that relates to how I "ended up" in Tucson, where I've been for about two and a half years. I'd lived in the northeastern part of the United States almost my whole life, and until about 14 years ago, I hadn't even known that a place like Tucson really existed. I came here on a brief vacation when my two now-teenage sons were still in preschool, and something magical happened: A seed got planted. It was the seed of possibility, a wondrous little spark of what might someday be.

I fell in love with Tucson, this jewel of a city in the blooming Sonoran desert, surrounded on all sides by mountains that are visible from almost anywhere. That December, as my husband and I hiked in the easily accessible peaks, it was 60 degrees and sunny. The birds were chirping up a storm, and I was shedding layers of clothing. The saguaro cacti towered all around me, and I felt the presence of the spirits of the ancestors that Native Americans believe reside in the plants.

Tucson is the only city in Arizona that has a medical school, and no matter where people live in the community, they can easily get to the school and its hospital complex. There's a Jewish community here, which matters to me, and an openness to holistic thinking about life and human well-being that isn't nearly as prevalent as it ought to be in our world. Tucson reaches out and grabs you if you're meant to be here. And that December, lo those many years ago, it grabbed *me*.

But I had a full outpatient psychiatric practice in Philadelphia. I was involved with a lot of folks, committed to seeing them through the long healing journey to wellness. And my husband had a busy urogynecology practice of his own. He couldn't readily leave it, and he had no interest in doing so anyway. "Tucson is way too hot in the summer," he told me. My folks were in the Northeast and were unable or unwilling to move. I was their main support at the time.

But the power of possibility spoke to me on that visit, and it wouldn't quit. So when I got back to Philadelphia, I contacted the Arizona medical-licensing board. Believing that I was someday meant to move to Tucson, I became licensed to practice here. And without knowing for sure if I'd ever come, I regularly renewed my license. There

was something about paying my 400-plus dollars each time ¦ arrived that was about living in possibility. I never questioned m̥ or desire to keep doing it; I just wrote my check and sent it off.

Meanwhile, I maintained a busy psychiatric practice in Phi phia, where I saw patients for 45 hours a week, year after year. B time went by, I became increasingly distressed about how broken models of care and intervention are. I kept helping people recover graduate from treatment who, before meeting me, had been stuc a never-ending cycle, searching for solutions and getting nowher felt the need to share what I was learning about the power and w of whole-person healing. I wanted to assist the myriad individu like you, whom I might never have the opportunity to meet as a sol practitioner.

I realized that I needed to start writing, teaching, and speakinç publicly to do this. But I couldn't pursue that and maintain a full-time clinical practice. So as each one of my patients graduated, I kept the slot that had been theirs open in my schedule. I didn't take on new patients. Eventually, I had enough time available to write *There's Always Help; There's Always Hope,* in which I recorded some of my patients' stories.

There was an amazing side benefit to making that dramatic and conscious change in my clinical practice: My work no longer tied me to Philadelphia! During that time, my mother died, and my father would have gone anywhere with me. And it just so happened that my husband had given up clinical work some years before—a casualty of the rising cost of medical-malpractice insurance, coupled with the decline in reimbursement for patient care. Unable to make a living in medicine, he'd taken a job in industry. While committed to his work, he was no longer tethered to Philadelphia either.

One day when Rick came home from work, we sat together in our living room to talk. It was a cold, gray winter day. Ice had covered the ground for weeks, and I'd been unable to take my daily walk outside for at least a month. "I really hate it here," I told him. "And I don't want to live in this area for the rest of my life. The kids [we now had four] are all at a reasonable enough point in their education to change schools without too much disruption. I'd like to go to Tucson over their spring break to research what it might be like to live there. The kids can visit

the schools they would go to; and we can explore the Jewish community, look at job options, houses, whatever. Let's see if it's possible for us to move there—if we're willing and ready to leap into something new. We'll have to do it this summer or wait until the boys both finish high school."

The passage of time brings about wondrous things. My husband sat in rapt attention and listened to me, as tears poured down my cheeks. "I'm ready to do that now, too," he said. "Let's go and see how we feel. I can imagine making a life there. I surely haven't been able to experience the life I thought I'd be having here, so I'm willing to check it out."

You, dear reader, know the end of this story, because I've told you that I live in Tucson now. But I want to share how clear it became that following my hunch, trusting my gut sense, and choosing to believe in the power of possibility enabled me to actualize what *was meant to be.*

We came to Tucson over spring break, and the kids immediately fell in love with this place. As soon as our plane landed and we began walking through the airport, the magic took hold. The sun was setting, and as we looked out the windows while walking toward baggage claim, we saw mountains everywhere. The sky glowed a gorgeous red, yellow, and orange.

The children gasped and—each seemingly more moved than the others—said, "It's awesome, Mom! Let's move here." Within the next few days, they visited the schools they might attend, and they each had a positive experience. All four were willing to make the change. My husband and I found a house to buy within two days, sold our Pennsylvania home for more than the asking price in just 24 hours on the market, and made the contact that ultimately led to my husband's current job. Rick and I returned to Philadelphia with a very deep sense that this was *meant to be.*

Today is January 16th. At sunrise I started my day off walking a path that I often follow. As I hiked up the steep hill around the corner from my home, I watched the sun rise over the mountains and listened to the birds sing as they darted from the saguaros to the mesquite trees to the palo verdes all around me. The air was crisp and cool for Tucson—winter mornings in the desert are awesome. The temperature was probably about 55 degrees when I started out, but as the sun rose,

the air warmed quickly. You can't help but feel it. Living here means you're immersed in nature—it's part of the magic of this place.

This morning as I crested the hill, I found myself thinking, *I love Tucson.* I thought back to that time in my life many years before when the city reached up and grabbed me in its loving arms. Had I not listened to the call, trusted in the power of possibility, and been willing to be patient and brave, I'd still be living in Pennsylvania, and I wasn't happy there. So here I am, living my dream, all because I was willing to trust in the Power of the Possible. If I can do it, so can you!

I'd like you to begin thinking about your hopes, prayers, and wishes for yourself. What do you want to see happen? What would you like to imagine could come to pass? I urge you to suspend your disbelief. Almost anything is possible; almost nothing is *im*possible. Let everything that comes into your mind, body, and spirit matter. Each message is there for a reason. Make notes of what you wish for here or on another sheet of paper.

_____

_____

_____

Perhaps you hope for inner peace, more free time, a life partner, children, career success, self-acceptance, self-love, good health, financial security, joy, a pet, a garden, or a dwelling that really feels like home. Whatever it is, it's possible . . . but you may not believe that. You most likely tell yourself "impossible" things such as: *Get real, Who are you kidding,* and *That will never happen.* You probably cut yourself off from realizing your dreams before you even get started naming them. We all do that sometimes.

Devote some thought to how you shut down your wishes for your life. How do you extinguish hope? What do you say?

_____

_____

_____

When you live the Power of the Possible, you banish your naysay-ers, your inner critics, and your doom-and-gloom voices. You work to identify them and then stop them in their tracks by using tools such as the thought-stopping technique and affirmations described in previ-ous chapters. If, for example, you don't know with absolute certainty that you can't find a life partner, then you must *stop it* whenever you hear yourself say, "I can't." Instead, you must say, "It's possible that I will," and step fully into doing whatever must be done to actualize that possibility. It might involve online dating, letting your friends know that you're looking, or participating in social activities with other like-minded individuals. It could mean giving the people you meet more of a chance than you do now, adjusting your expectations of others, or challenging your notions of romantic love. You *must trust that it is possible* for you to find a life partner if you really want one, and then do whatever you can to make it happen.

Living in the Power of the Possible means many things. While the concept stays the same, it may take time to recognize how to apply it to a series of different situations. Since you probably need to practice bringing this idea into your life, I'd like to walk you through a group of ten possibility questions, with anecdotes that demonstrate the lessons of the first five. As you read and consider the possibilities presented, ask *yourself* the questions, too. Think about how you can apply the teachings in each section to your own story.

Consider-the-Possibilities Exercise

1. Is it possible that you're wonderful just the way you are, and that your *self-doubt* or *anxiety* is the problem? I was seeing Fred in my office for a consultation. He'd just finished his first semester of college and was home on winter break. His dad, a colleague of mine, had asked me to see the young man because he'd had a tough term. A straight-A and honor student in high school, he'd found the rigor of college courses and the lack of structure quite challenging. He'd done fine (his grades were mostly B's), but he was convinced that he wasn't smart enough to make it in college. He didn't even know if he wanted to go back.

As Fred talked about his experiences at school, I began to see a pattern. He'd started each course with optimism and openness, but he'd gotten a B on the first test or paper in each class. Although he hadn't yet learned how to succeed in college at the level he was accustomed to in high school, he was immediately devastated. He started telling himself, *I'm not smart enough to excel,* and convinced himself that he was right. He chose not to go for the extra help that all the freshmen were encouraged to make use of because he was sure it wouldn't make a difference. Although he made it through the rest of the semester without his performance suffering even more, he found the whole experience so overwhelming and demoralizing that he didn't want to return.

Fred struck me as a very bright young man. When he described the courses he'd taken during his senior year of high school—in which he'd excelled—I could tell that he was a brilliant kid. But he'd never before had to work at his studies to do well, and he clearly didn't know how to do so.

"Fred," I said, "you're a gifted student who can do phenomenally well in college, but you have to learn how to study. You've never had so much work to do on your own time, so few hours in the classroom, and such a need to be focused in your study hours. I really believe that your self-doubt, and consequent unwillingness to go for coaching help, is the problem.

"Would you be willing to start the next semester believing that *it is possible for you to excel?* Will you sign up for study-skills coaching right away and give yourself every opportunity to succeed? I'd be glad to see you again if you have trouble improving your performance, but I doubt that will happen. What do you think?"

Fred decided to trust my assessment of the situation enough to do what I recommended. We shook hands, and I wished him well.

Some months passed and I hadn't heard from Fred. Then one spring morning I ran into his dad in the hospital where we both worked. "I can't thank you enough," he said. "Fred did exactly what you suggested. He's getting straight A's again, but more important, he's excited about being in school. And he was so moved by the power of your lesson that he decided to teach study skills to incoming freshmen. He goes around the dorms sharing his story to get his fellow students to sign up for help."

Grateful to hear of these developments, I told Fred's dad, "I only suggested that your son banish his self-doubt and consider the possibility that he could excel. I'm so glad he chose to do that."

Consider whether your self doubt or anxiety is the problem. Is it possible that you're wonderful just the way you are?

2. Is it possible that the little things you worry about all the time aren't nearly as important as you think they are? You probably have an immediate "yes" response to this question, as almost all of us relate to this dynamic. I believe that the universality of this problem is the main reason that the book *Don't Sweat the Small Stuff . . . and It's All Small Stuff* is such a success. We all "sweat stuff" a lot and think our worries matter. But we also know deep down inside that we're often spinning our wheels, wasting energy, and focusing on insignificant issues.

When I was about 18 years old, I escorted groups of adults two, three, and four times my age to Eastern Europe and what was then the Soviet Union. I worked for a U.S.-based tour-packaging company, and my job was to travel with the groups and make sure that everything ran smoothly. I worked with the local city guides, hotels, airlines, and so on. For some reason, I found very little of it overwhelming, but I did always worry, *What if we get to Moscow or Leningrad and the local guide with the bus doesn't meet me at the airport? This could be a big problem.*

You see, in the USSR at that time, the government owned and ran all tourist operations—including the hotels and local tour-guide agencies. For reasons of "security," tour groups weren't told where they'd be staying in advance. The Intourist guide who met us at the airport would tell us what hotel we'd be going to and have a bus ready to take us there. *How will I possibly know where to go and what to do with my group of 30 to 40 tourists if no local help appears?* I would worry . . . a lot!

And then, guess what? It happened! I got to Moscow with 35 travelers, and no guide appeared. It turned out that I had no time to worry. I designated one group member as the leader, parked all my tourists around him, and told him to keep everyone together until I returned. I'd find out what to do.

And off I went. I quickly found an Intourist representative in the airport who got on the phone immediately. In rapid-fire Russian, he sorted out what had happened, secured a bus for us, ascertained where we were meant to stay, and told me that our guide would be at the hotel by the time we got there.

In no time flat, my group was en route to our accommodations—and no one besides me and the driver had any idea that there'd even been the slightest glitch in the plans. As I sat at the front of the bus, microphone in hand, pointing out and describing the sights along the way, I realized that my long-standing worry had been much ado about nothing.

Today, whenever I hear myself or any of my patients say, "What will I do if . . . ?" and then go on to describe some worry about *what might be,* I reply, "We'll deal with it when we get there." Reminding myself and those I serve that there will be a solution when the time comes is deeply comforting. It allows the worrier to relax and let go.

Consider whether the small things that you worry about all the time are as important or worrisome as you make them out to be. Is it possible that you're more capable than you give yourself credit for?

3. Is it possible that your assumption about what will happen is wrong? We so often play the role of prophet, convinced that we know what will happen when we actually have no reason to believe that our predictions are correct. "I can't do that because . . ." we say. The latter part of our sentence is, of course, some statement about what will absolutely happen if we do whatever it is.

My patient Denise had finally agreed to meet with a sales rep, Jack, who kept hounding her. She couldn't keep saying no, but she had no intention of buying anything from him. Beyond that, she was very busy and didn't want to spend an hour over coffee with him. "Well, just tell him the truth," I told her. "You're not in a position to place an order with him at this point, and you can't spare the time."

"I can't do that," Denise said. "I'll hurt his feelings. And I see him in social situations."

The two of us began to explore her response. "Is it possible you're wrong?" I asked. "Jack is a salesman, so he's used to being turned down like this. Pushing to get together is what he does to make and close deals. But he, like everyone in his profession, knows that 'No, thank you' comes with the territory. What makes you think he's so fragile?"

As Denise sat with the question, she realized that she could, of course, be wrong. Empowered to set the boundaries she needed in order to take care of herself, she called Jack to cancel the meeting.

"No problem," he replied. "I'm sure we'll have other opportunities to get together in the future."

Denise was impressed with his resiliency. "I learned a big lesson," she said.

Consider whether your assumptions about what will happen are wrong. How often do you play prophet? Is it possible that you hold yourself back by assuming you know things that you really don't?

4. Is it possible that you're attributing an incorrect motivation to someone else's behavior and suffering as a result? One day when Georgette came for her regular psychotherapy session, she said, "I need to talk to you about what happened last night." As she tried to complete her next sentence, she began to cry.

"It's okay, Georgette," I said. "You're clearly upset, but that's why you need to talk. When you're ready, just start telling me what happened."

Within a minute, she calmed down enough to share her deep pain of rejection. An old friend named Violet had been withdrawing more and more, and the previous night's events had been the culmination of Georgette's growing distress. Violet was at home but wouldn't come to the phone when my client called and reached Violet's husband. He said that she "didn't want to talk."

I asked Georgette to describe the history of the friendship. Before her move away two years earlier, she and Violet had lived in the same city for many years. They spent most mornings working out at the same gym, eating breakfast together, talking on the phone, and taking trips. They were close buddies who shared the details of their lives on a regular basis.

But in the last several years, they'd grown more and more apart. Georgette would reach out and call Violet, get together with her when she returned to her old town, and invite her to come visit her in her new home. But Violet initiated few contacts and never paid Georgette a visit.

My client began to feel hurt. She said to herself, *Maybe she doesn't really care about me the way I thought she did. I don't know what I'm doing wrong.* She carried this pain forward. Then, when Violet was too wiped out to come to the phone that night, she cracked, and all the pain burst forth.

But as we began to examine the relationship history, a lightbulb went off for Georgette. When I asked her to tell me how Violet was at maintaining long-distance relationships, Georgette realized that her friend didn't do that at all! When people left, they were no longer part of her life. She was great at maintaining intimacy with those she saw on a regular basis, but she was awful at extending herself and maintaining connections across time and space.

Her withdrawal wasn't personal; she was just being how she always was. Georgette's move had destabilized the relationship. It probably couldn't continue as it had been, but it had nothing to do with issues of caring or my client doing something wrong.

"I feel better already," Georgette said upon realizing that she'd attributed incorrect meaning to inevitable developments in the relationship. She left feeling more prepared to deal with Violet, and was more assured of her own value to her many other friends.

Consider how often you attribute incorrect motivation to the behavior of others and suffer as a result. Is it possible that your assumptions about why people behave as they do are incorrect? Might you feel better off if you stopped doing that?

5. Is it possible that your "failure," setback, or loss is really an opportunity in disguise? How many people do you know who had to lose their jobs in order to find their passion? What about those who had to fail in their own businesses in order to discover that they work best when someone else establishes and maintains the corporate structure? Are you close to anyone whose addictive illnesses had to escalate to the point that they hit rock bottom and lose everything in order to find and reclaim their lives? How many folks do you know who needed to get divorced in order to find true love or experience a home robbery in order to become grateful for the gift of continued life? Think about the individuals who have found profound meaning in life only because they're helping others cope with the traumas that they've endured themselves.

Have you ever experienced a business loss that you thought would do you in, only to emerge better off financially? Perhaps you've lost a friendship, only to discover how damaging it had been to you; or become clinically depressed, unduly anxious, or physically ill because you were pushing yourself beyond your limit and needed to learn how to take better care of yourself.

Have you ever gotten to the point where you felt that you couldn't handle one more loss or setback, only to discover a strength within yourself or your relationships that you never knew existed? Have your relationships with others grown deeper because you were touched by a serious illness or the death of a loved one? Have you ever been hurt so badly by someone that you never wanted to deal with that person again, but found that the two of you grew closer once you worked together to repair the wound?

Have you ever found healing in *the way* that a parent, sibling, or friend died? Have you grown closer to your children as a result of being there through their countless temper tantrums, or learned how to live your dreams by studying the parts of your life that have been such a nightmare?

I'm sure you said yes to some of the questions you just read. I hope that you relate to the expression "Whenever a door closes, a window opens." Our lives are constant manifestations of this fact: We're denied admission to our first-choice college and meet our soul mate at our second-choice school. We're devastated by infertility and adopt a child who becomes the light of our life. We can't afford to live in the community we most desire but make lifelong friends with the neighbors we do have. Perhaps our car breaks down and a stranger helps us out.

Whenever a door closes, a window opens. If you really believe in this, you'll be awestruck by how frequently you see it manifest. But you do really have to look for it.

Make a list of at least three times in your life when you've seen a door shut and a window open—a loss led to a gain, a hurt called forth a joy. Then *consider* how often you focus on your failures, setbacks, and losses and feel overwhelmed by them. Is it possible that you're looking at your painful experiences in the wrong way? Might they actually be opportunities in disguise? How would it change your life if you started searching for the window each time a door closed in your face?

I think you're getting the hang of the "Consider-the-Possibilities" exercise. As you read each of the following questions, start creating your own examples to illustrate each concept. You now know, of course, that for each "Is it possible?" question, the answer is yes. It *is* possible, so prove it!

6. Is it possible for you to outlive the odds? Could you have a spontaneous remission if you develop a supposedly fatal illness? Might you prove the experts wrong?

7. Is it possible that being forced to confront your own mortality—whether through cancer, diabetes, addiction, depression, heart disease, or the like—can teach you how to live?

8. Is it possible that you deserve to heal? Are you meant to experience fulfillment? Do you have gifts the world needs you to share?

9. Is it possible that your enemies can become your friends? Do more people care about you than you realize? Are you loving and lovable?

10. Is it possible for you to take charge of your emotional life? Can you master a ten-step program designed to do so and thus live your dreams?

ADDITIONAL STRATEGIES

You *can* take charge of your emotional life, and you've come a long way in doing so. You're deep into the ninth step already! In working this chapter's concept—live in the Power of the Possible—you've come to understand the importance of believing in your dreams, quieting and challenging your inner critics and naysayers, affirming yourself, continuing to ask if it's possible to look at a situation differently, and making sure that you search for the windows that will appear whenever doors close in your life. I'd like to offer you five additional guidelines to follow as you propel yourself into the wonderful world of possibility:

1. Monitor the company you keep.
2. Share your dreams.
3. Cultivate patience.
4. Visualize yourself already there.
5. Use varied-volume affirmations.

As you read the description of each idea, imagine yourself using the tool. All of these techniques are readily available to you for your immediate use!

1. Monitor the company you keep. Some folks heal us, while others unsettle us. People who are loving, accepting, encouraging, upbeat, and optimistic are most apt to inspire us and nurture our spirits. Those who are critical, negative, and pessimistic are most likely to destabilize us.

To stay in touch with the power of possibility, surround yourself with individuals who nurture, calm, inspire, and encourage you. Keep far away from those who tell you, "You can't succeed," "You're not good enough," or "Bad things are bound to happen."

Pay attention to how you feel in the company of different folks. Notice when your energy picks up—when you feel excited, at peace, at home, and at ease. Also, register when you become anxious, have a less-than feeling, or are overcome by hopelessness. Observe your body language when it somehow tells you *I like that person,* and when it says *Beware* or *I need space.* Your inner wisdom is brilliant, and your body is always talking to you. It knows where you can thrive and where you'll be held back. Listen to it, and honor its messages.

For example, I'm immediately unsettled by those who are critical, pessimistic, preoccupied with themselves, or who always seem to think that they know what's best for me better than I do. As soon as I begin to feel anxious around someone, I look long and hard at what's going on. I ask myself, *Is there something about associating with this individual that's destructive for me?* If the answer comes up yes, I set a boundary as soon as possible. I cut my losses (no matter how great) and find a way to walk away.

By contrast, if I'm drawn to someone—that is, excited, energized, or joyful in their company—I consider the healing power of associating with them. If it becomes clear that they nurture me somehow, and the opportunity allows, I try to build more of a relationship with them.

I honor my body messages at work and in play. I hire and partner with those who support my efforts to make a difference in the world, and run for the hills from those I believe interfere with my mission. I surround myself with friends who want to know what I'm doing, believe in me, and want to see me succeed. I don't allow folks that doubt me to become or remain my friends.

Tip: Pay attention to what your body's telling you. Surround yourself with those who believe in you. Avoid spending time in the company of anyone who makes you feel anxious, self-critical, negative, or hopeless. Ask yourself: *Does this person help me live in possibility, or push me into impossible thinking?* Monitor the company you keep, and make sure that your relationships support your Step 9 work.

2. Share your dreams. You may carry a silent dream for a long time, but until you give voice to your hope, it doesn't fully exist. And in that state, it can't be actualized. So you must share your hopes, wishes, dreams, and prayers. Living in possibility requires you to do that.

But whom should you tell? Who is safe? You sure don't want to hear that you're foolish, grandiose, or unrealistic, and lots of stuck-in-the-muck folks tell dreamers those things. So who's your ally? Look for someone who heals you and whose company you're drawn to, a person who has encouraged or supported you in the past. Perhaps it's a friend, relative, therapist, coach, or pastoral counselor.

Remember my story about how I "ended up" in Tucson? I would never have gotten here if I hadn't shared my dream with my husband and, in another way, with the Arizona medical-licensing board! The telling made the dream real. Once it existed with a life of its own, it could manifest.

Tip: Find someone who believes in you. If that means hiring a therapist or coach, do so. Share your hopes, dreams, prayers, and fears with that person. Let him or her help you banish all doubts. You can realize your dreams. This is positively possible!

3. Cultivate patience. This is a biggie. After all, there's a reason we all know the expression "Rome wasn't built in a day." We need to be reminded of the pace at which real change happens. When we're bothered by something or wish things were different, we want the situation to change overnight. *I want what I want, and I want it now!* we seem to be screaming inside. We're unrealistic and impatient. Although we may know that true growth, substantial change, or actual transformation takes a long time, we don't really get that. We expect miracles and often get down on ourselves when we fall short of our crazy ideas.

When this happens, we feel like failures, become hopeless, and quickly give up on our attempts to effect change. Think about it: How long do most people stick to their New Year's resolutions, diets, and debt-busting plans? How many describe their brief efforts by saying, "I tried that, but it didn't work"?

We lose perspective quickly and need to be reminded to hang in there. It *is* possible to effect change, but it takes time.

Tip: When you notice self-doubt, hopelessness, or despair creeping in, cultivate patience in yourself by challenging your negativity with the questions: *Is it possible that I'm making more progress than I can see? Might I be asking too much of myself?*

Remind yourself that Rome *wasn't* built in a day. It took you a long time to get where you are now. You've carried certain ideas with you and enacted your particular behavior patterns for quite a while. It may be some time before you see a substantial alteration in yourself, but change is possible, and if you hang in there long enough, it *will* come.

4. Visualize yourself already there. The more we see ourselves where we want to end up, the more likely we are to believe in our potential to get there. Think back to the story of Carol, the runner who was able to qualify for the Olympic team after injuring her leg because she trained her mind—and thus her body—to be there.

So often we cut off the possibility of achieving what matters to us by refusing to consider that it could happen. But what if each time you thought, *I'd like to get to know Jim better* or *I'd love to own my own flower store,* you chose not to silence the desire with a *No way* response. What if you just started imagining yourself socializing with Jim or arranging flowers in your new shop? How might you feel if you daydreamed yourself into being where you wanted to go? Do you think this exercise would make your goals easier to achieve?

Most people who achieve great feats use this strategy, whether they're athletes, entrepreneurs, performers, or sales reps. Time and time again, they'll tell you that the secret to their success was the decision to see themselves, in their mind's eye, succeeding. It makes sense, doesn't it? If we can envision something, we're more apt to try to realize it. And if we work toward it, we're more likely to make it real. It seems pretty basic when you get down to it.

Tip: Visualize yourself where you want to be, whether or not you trust in your ability to get there. This exercise will nurture your belief in the possibility of realizing your dreams. And that, of course, is the first step to actualizing them.

5. Use varied-volume affirmations. Here's the affirmation you're going to use to practice this technique: *I can take charge.* To begin, stand up and say the affirmation out loud five times. The first time, you'll use a loud voice and a lot of emphasis only when you say the first word, *I.* So you'll say: *I can take charge*—where the underlined word is loud. The second time you say the affirmation, you make the second word loud, and so on. Your first four affirmations will be like this:

1st time:	*I can take charge!*
2nd time:	*I CAN take charge!*
3rd time:	*I can TAKE charge!*
4th time:	*I can take CHARGE!*

Then you will say *all four* words in a loud voice and with a lot of emphasis: *I CAN TAKE CHARGE!*

Stand up now (unless you're in the car, a public library, or some such place) and do this exercise. You'll feel an amazing surge of energy and sense of hope when you're through. It's awesome! I often use this tool when working with large audiences to quickly demonstrate the Power of Possibility. When hundreds of people do this together, the energy is unbelievable. Everyone feels empowered by it!

You can use any affirmation you want for this exercise, but it works best with short sentences (three or four words is best) and single-syllable words. Also, it falls flat with an ending word such as *it* or *so*. Try to finish with an action word, such as *heal: I can heal!*

Tip: Pick a varied-volume affirmation statement that speaks to you; use one of the examples I've provided or create your own. Try using this technique every day for a few weeks. You'll be amazed by the power it has to keep you living in possibility.

You've come to the end of Step 9. You're amazing! You've learned so much and grown so beautifully thus far. I'm really proud of you. I'm impressed with your willingness to learn, your persistence in staying with the process, and your commitment to keep on going. I hope you feel as good as I do about what you've accomplished.

In your last and final step, you'll learn how to nurture your spirit. I'm sure you'll enjoy the stories and exercises in Step 10.

STEP 10

Nurture Your Spirit

Welcome to Step 10! In this chapter, you'll focus on bringing spiritual practices—whether faith-based or not—into your Take-Charge program. The relationship between spirituality, health, and emotional well-being has been understood for countless generations. In many ancient cultures, healers were the spiritual leaders of their communities. Only recently (as you learned in Step 4) has our biomedical model of healing and treatment gotten so disconnected from crucial teachings and enduring wisdom.

Step 10 is a particularly powerful part of your Take-Charge program because it's all-encompassing. You see, the biological interventions—such as the medications and herbal remedies that you worked on in Steps 1 through 4—operate predominantly on the inner-limbic emotional areas of your brain in order to effect change. By contrast, the cognitive interventions—such as thought stopping and reprogramming brain circuits covered in Step 6—work on the outer cortical areas of your brain to bring about transformation. But with spiritual pursuits, you get a double benefit.

These systems and practices work on the deep emotional brain and its outer cortical structures. All spiritual traditions include ideas, beliefs, values, and philosophies about life. When you immerse yourself in those teachings, you process and live them through your *thinking, cortical* brain. But these faith systems also include actions, such as meditation, song, prayer, yogic breathing, and postures. When you engage in those activities, you involve your *deep emotional* brain to bring about a response. Involving yourself in spiritual pursuits on a consistent basis is therefore a particularly powerful way to take charge of your emotional life.

I believe that spirituality is fundamental to your mental and physical health, but I want you to understand what I mean when I say *spirituality.* I believe that spirituality involves the meaning and purpose of existence. It includes notions of a higher calling, your sense of connection to something bigger and grander than yourself, and the belief that we're meant to share our gifts to help enrich one another. It answers the question "Why am I here?" and includes the realms of religion, mysticism, meditation, and the sacred. It's the root of life and the source of the infinite within each one of us.

Spirituality encompasses the experience of connection and oneness that unites all creatures—that *healing force* that reverberates between two or more people, or between a single soul and the universe. This energy is also sometimes apparent in an astonishing moment when we feel that the wisdom of the world has been revealed to us. Spirituality is the whole, which is infinitely greater than the sum of its parts. It's the holy or the miraculous in the mundane.

This doesn't necessarily have to involve organized religion. Many people are extremely religious, but they may not be spiritual; others are extraordinarily spiritual, but have no affiliation with a church, temple, or other congregation.

Whether you're a devout religious follower or not, your search for meaning can offer you a sense of hope and self-worth. If nothing else, your connection to the world can lift you out of yourself, shed new light upon the struggles you face, and offer you a momentary reprieve from those challenges. In a world as chaotic and complex as ours, it's certainly easy to lose your way; a sense of faith and purpose can be your guiding thread through this labyrinth.

You mustn't underestimate the power of spirituality when it comes to your physical, mental, and emotional well-being. I've personally seen the miraculous emerge from a tiny sliver of faith, and devastation take over when all hope was snuffed out. I've watched the power of love transform lives, and isolation and alienation destroy them. I've seen children excel when told that they're smart, and fail when told that they aren't. I've observed patients with hope survive illnesses that were thought to be fatal, and others in despair die of curable diseases.

And finally, I've experienced the healing power of love, hope, and acceptance in my own life. I've been lucky enough to learn how to offer these gifts to others. My faith in the value, purpose, and potential of each of my patients helps them heal; and by teaching them to see themselves in kind, they blossom.

In *Essential Spirituality,* Roger Walsh, M.D., Ph.D., demonstrates that each of the great spiritual traditions shares a common belief: The sacred and divine exists both within and around us. In his book, he does a wonderful job of showing the universality of that teaching. He put together the following statements—central messages that are clearly consistent over time and space:

- "The kingdom of heaven is within you. (Jesus, Christianity)"

- "Those who know themselves know their Lord. (Mohammad, Islam)"

- "He is in all, and all is in Him. (Judaism)"

- "Those who know completely their own nature, know heaven. (Mencius, Confucianism)"

- "In the depths of the soul, one sees the Divine, the One. (The Chinese *Book of Changes*)"

- "Atman [individual consciousness] and Brahman [universal consciousness] are one. (Hinduism)"

- "Look within, you are the Buddha. (Buddhism)"

His book is filled with practices you can use to awaken your heart and mind to this truth. I highly recommend his work as a way to cultivate healing through kindness, love, joy, peace, vision, wisdom, and generosity.

THE BENEFITS OF SPIRITUAL PRACTICES

Lots of studies have demonstrated the power of spiritual practices—such as yoga, prayer, meditation, and tai chi—to augment the healing response. People who engage in these activities regularly often live longer and healthier lives. You know from Step 4 that most Americans believe in God or some universal spirit. Gallup polls have shown this to be true of about 95 percent of us! Nearly 60 percent of respondents say religion is "very important" to them, and at least 54 percent believe in spiritual healing. Many pray for their own health or for the recovery of loved ones who are ill. Overwhelmingly, people believe that their prayers are answered.

All spiritual practices connect individuals to something larger than themselves. They also promote a positive worldview in which every person matters. They encourage self-love and caring for others, and prescribe the performance of acts of kindness: "Love your neighbor as yourself" or "Do unto others as you would have others do unto you." They validate the experience of suffering and offer perspective, hope, guidance, and support in negotiating life's challenges. Engaging in spiritual practices decreases the stress response—the fight-or-flight reaction—that releases cortisol and depresses the immune system. They allow our bodies to return to their innate self-healing states.

SPIRITUAL PRINCIPLES

The wisdom of spiritual teachings is enduring; its practices are clearly life affirming and enhancing. I personally believe that hope heals, prayer and other spiritual pursuits transform lives, and that anyone can find a spiritual home. In Step 10, you'll examine your spiritual history and work at creating your own spirit-care plan. You'll explore such topics as your beliefs about God and religion, what gives your life meaning, and where you can find support for what matters to you.

You'll examine your involvement in spiritual pursuits and consider what you might want to add or alter. This part of your Take-Charge program is crucial because spirituality is fundamental to physical and emotional health.

Before beginning your own exploratory work, please review the following list of spiritual principles. All of these beliefs are embodied in the Take-Charge program, and some of them will be familiar to you already. My comments on these concepts are italicized and in parentheses. As you read through these statements, think about which ones you already believe and live, which ones make sense to you but aren't active in your mind or behavior, and which ones you have trouble accepting could be true.

1. You're amazing, wondrous, and a piece of the divine—that is, you're enough, and you deserve to be free and well. *(Because I see you this way, I'm committed to helping you heal.)*

2. Your inner wisdom is brilliant; if something doesn't *feel* right, it isn't. *(My job is to help you find your personal right answers.)*

3. Your inner healer is looking for partners. *(That's why you're reading this book and working this program.)*

4. There's a reason for your symptoms, distress, or difficulty, and you can discover it. *(You've already identified much of what you need to know.)*

5. You're here for a reason and needed in the world. *(I need you as much as you need me.)*

6. What matters to you is of the utmost importance. *(What matters to you is what you're meant to express.)*

7. You can live the life you want and are meant to lead. *(Rumi, one of Islam's great mystics, taught: "Everyone has been made for some particular work, and the desire for that work has been put in our heart." Through the Take-Charge program, you'll find your place in the world.)*

8. Where there's a will, there's a way. *(I've found this to be true with every patient I've ever known. You're no different.)*

9. Although you may not understand "why" tragedy strikes, you can always learn from it and be transformed for good. *(I've never found the "Why me?" question to be helpful in trying to explain tragedy. But I've seen many people transcend devastation by trying to learn from it.)*

10. There's a right answer to every question, but it's always a *personal* right answer. *(My clinical work has taught me this.)*

11. There's a spiritual path that you're meant to travel—a spiritual home that's right for you—and you can find it. *(There's a place for you. You must look deep within yourself as you search the world around you to find your spot.)*

12. You're a blessed child of the universe. *(Whether you recognize it or not, you're blessed. We all are.)*

13. In giving, you receive. *(We're transformed, healed, and uplifted when we share.)*

14. There are no small acts of kindness. *(Think about how many times your day has been transformed by a simple compliment, a smile, or some other little nicety.)*

15. An attitude of gratitude transforms lives. *(Both feeling grateful and offering thanks heal us. The former affects the feeler, while the latter alters both parties!)*

16. You can take charge of your emotional life. *(I'm sure you're seeing this reality play out already.)*

17. Love is *almost* all you need! *(While love is crucial, it can't substitute for guidance and direction. You need all three!)*

18. You're never alone. *(Reach out for help, and you'll be answered.)*

What came into your mind as you read the 18 spiritual principles and my comments? Did you identify with any, some, or many of them? Were my comments helpful? Record your thoughts below or on a separate piece of paper.

_____

_____

_____

Because my life and work have shown me how fundamental faith is to the recovery process, I'm committed to helping you bring the spiritual dimension into your Take-Charge plan. You may already have a deep sense of faith, trust, or spirituality but have no idea how to use it to support yourself in your journey to heal. By contrast, you may be skeptical of religion and spirituality and feel challenged by the mere notion that faith heals or that belief matters when it comes to your mental well-being. I've worked with individuals from both ends of the spectrum, and I can help you no matter where you are.

Interestingly, it's been my experience that many sufferers who believe in God or have a profound sense of spirituality don't know how to apply the teachings and practices of their faith in their own healing. For example, many folks believe that a piece of the divine resides in every human being but still see themselves as worthless. Do you relate to this conflict?

These two beliefs do not fit together; they can't logically coexist. So if you have a sense of faith, your Step 10 work may focus on challenging your self-concept with what you know to be spiritually true about humankind, or it might involve learning how to use your traditions more directly to enhance your healing. Later in this chapter, you'll read Miguel's story. This deeply religious man learned how to use prayer phrases to take charge of his emotional life and heal his trauma. You can learn a lot from studying his journey.

If you question the meaning of existence, doubt that a higher power exists, or feel deeply disconnected from spiritual principles and concepts in your life, your Step 10 work will be different. You'll need to nurture a sense of hope in what's possible, increase your involvement in activities that offer the opportunity for human connection and sharing, and begin to explore ways to find meaning in your life. Later in this chapter, you'll also read Juliette's story. When she came to me, she doubted God's existence and saw no role for spiritual pursuits in healing. But she ultimately found her anxiety disorder transformed when she added activities to her Take-Charge program that fostered connection, service, inner peace, and meaning. You'll learn a lot from her tale, too!

In order to help you figure out where you are on your spiritual path and what you might need to do to nurture it, I've included some questions for reflection. As you go through the "Spiritual-Assessment" exercise, reflect on the meaning and purpose of existence. What's your notion of a higher power or God? What gifts do you have that you're meant to share? What matters to you? Why do you think you're here? If you happen to have had a devout upbringing, what did you learn from it? What was constructive and what wasn't? For example, did you learn about a loving, compassionate God or a punishing one Who's out to get you for your sins? Are you able to use helpful religious teachings in your life? Can you let go of difficult or harmful messages? What do you do with what you've learned?

As you go through the additional questions on the next page, document whatever comes to mind. This will help you figure out where you need to start your Step 10 work. I want you to know that there are no objective right or wrong answers here, only those that are *personally* correct. You can feel moved and uplifted when you're singing in a choir, climbing a mountain, donating your time to a charitable organization, or sitting in a quiet chapel. Your spiritual connection can take many wonderful forms.

Spiritual-Assessment Exercise

- What do I value most in life?

- What are my most precious memories? What are my dearest belongings?

- Whom do I respect the most? Why?

- Where, when, and with whom do I feel the most calm or at peace?

- What words heal me?

- What words harm me?

- Do I have a spiritual home? If so, where? If not, why not?

- Do I see myself as a child of the universe? If so, do I treat myself like one? If not, why not?

- Do I show myself as much love as I show my children, pets, partners, friends, relatives, and neighbors? If not, why not?

- Do I offer to help others?

- Do I allow myself to ask for assistance when I need it?

- Do I treat my body like the physical temple that houses my soul? If not, why not?

- Do I give and receive love with a full heart?

- Do I act from a place of self-love and affection for others?

- Do I allow judgment and criticism to rule my life?

- Do I approach pain with humility and a desire to learn from it?

- Do I give thanks for the many blessings in my life? Do I even know what they are?

- Do I take the time to watch the sunrise or sunset, to smell a flower, or to say a prayer?

- Do I strive for peace and harmony, or would I rather be right?

- Do I say "I'm sorry" often enough? Too much?

- Do I believe in magic, miracles, and wonder?

- Do I allow myself to experience pure joy?

- Do I give myself permission to be silly, playful, and creative?

- Do I allow myself to laugh and cry enough?

- Do I hear my spirit when it sings? Do I allow myself to dance to its music?

- At the end of my days, what do I hope to be remembered for? Am I living a life that supports that vision? If not, why is that?

- Do I surround myself with people who nurture my spirit? If not, why don't I?

- Do I spend the bulk of my time pursuing what matters most to me? If not, what gets in the way?

- Am I generous with my time, money, self, and gifts? If not, why not? Am I afraid that they'll get used up?

Each time I read through the questions in this exercise, I feel moved. In fact, when I do healing workshops, I often have an attendee read the list aloud to the group before we journal or share with one another. By the time the last question is read, most people feel deeply touched. There's something very powerful—almost meditative or prayerlike—that happens when we step into contemplation of meaning, beauty, self-love, love of others, and the sacred. We're transformed as we explore questions of purpose, wisdom, humility, and gratitude; we're reminded of what truly matters.

Please take some time to reflect on your reactions to the "Spiritual-Assessment" exercise. What did you learn from it? What might you want to explore or change?

_____

_____

_____

I suggest that you take time to write more extensively than you may have in earlier parts of the book, perhaps in a journal or on your computer. Why? Because figuring out where you are on your spiritual path and what makes sense for you to do for personal growth is an exercise in deep self-exploration and reflection. While I can give you some suggestions about what to consider and teach you how to approach particular types of challenges, you'll need to find your unique spiritual path "home."

To emphasize this point, I'd like to paraphrase the wise words of one of my favorite authors, Kahlil Gibran in *The Prophet: No one can teach you anything but what is already asleep in the dawning of your own knowledge. . . . Each one of us must be alone in our knowledge of God and in our understanding of the earth.* Meaningfulness is deeply personal. I can lead you to the doorway of your journey, and I can even give you some directions to follow along your way. But ultimately, you'll need to wrestle with your own demons and find your own personal path to purpose, wholeness, and maybe even God.

I'd like to share a few stories with you to illustrate how you can use spiritual beliefs and practices to transform challenge. In the first tale, you'll see how I helped a religious man use his faith to overcome a sleep/trauma problem. Then you'll learn how a woman who lacked faith in God learned to use spiritual questions (about meaningfulness and purpose) and pursuits (acts of charity) to transform her anxiety disorder. As you read these stories, think about how they relate to you and your Take-Charge needs. Are you religious? Do you believe in God? Do you know how to use your faith to support your own healing? Or do you lack faith in God? Do you have a sense that some spiritual values, ideas, approaches, or practices could help you? Do you know how to use them for wellness? Let yourself learn from the experiences of others.

FAITH HEALS: MIGUEL'S STORY

Miguel, a deeply religious man of 68, asked me to help him overcome a sleep problem. He'd immigrated to the United States as a young man to escape persecution in his birth country. He'd made a good life here and was grateful to God for his salvation. He attended church regularly and prayed several times each day.

But several years before meeting me, Miguel had begun having terrible dreams every single night that would awaken him—usually screaming—and scare him so much that he was often unable to fall back to sleep. He'd been to many doctors and therapists, but nothing had helped. He'd tried some sleep medicines, but they made him groggy and confused. He was at his wit's end, and wondered if there was something I could do.

As you know by now, I needed to hear Miguel's story to figure out how to understand his problem and determine the route to his recovery. So, I asked him to tell me his tale. We began to explore questions such as: What was the content of his dreams? Had he ever had similar problems? Did he suffer from any psychiatric condition? What was happening in his life when the sleep problem began? And so on.

I learned that as a child, Miguel had witnessed and suffered great trauma. His life had often been in danger. He saw many he knew and loved die. After coming to the U.S., it had taken him some time to stop reliving the horror of his childhood, but he had been well for many, many years.

Although he hadn't realized that there could be a connection, he'd written a memoir several years before I met him. It won't surprise you to learn that writing the book required him to revisit the trauma of his past, and in doing so, it came alive again. His body memories became activated, and he began to have nightmares of being in danger, unable to escape.

So, first of all, I helped Miguel understand why he was having a reemergence of his symptoms—that is, his body was back in the past. Then I taught him what to do to heal. When he awoke in fear, I told him to remind himself that he was now safe. The dream was history coming alive—but the trauma was over. He was at no current risk.

As I explained all this, something told me that Miguel needed more than the explanation and affirmation to combat the reappearance of his severe-trauma experience. So I asked him if there were any prayers or teachings from his religion that he might utter when he awoke in fear—phrases that could soothe him.

Miguel had never thought of using his faith in such a specific, self-healing way, but he immediately remembered a prayer phrase that he could use. It spoke of the role of God as the healer—something along the lines of "My Lord heals me," as I recall. I suggested that he say those words over and over when he awoke. I believed that because they had such meaning and power for him, they'd settle his nervous system and allow him to drop off again.

By the time I saw Miguel the next week, he was sleeping through the night. He'd begun using the affirmation and prayer phrase immediately. The first night he'd awoken several times but was able to fall back to sleep each time. As the week went on, he awoke fewer and fewer times, and he was able to drift off again quicker and quicker. After eight nights, he was no longer waking up at all. His faith, in a sense, had healed him.

Yes, he did need to understand the reason for his troubles and begin an affirmation practice to combat old fears. We can't minimize the role of these other steps in his recovery. But the bulk of his cure involved a very specific use of his prayer practice. Once he learned how to apply the teachings and words of his faith to his particular challenge—in just the right way and at just the right time—he quickly transformed a problem that he'd been dealing with for years. This story is a great example of the idea that faith heals, don't you think?

Do you relate to Miguel's story? How might you benefit from applying the teachings of your belief system to your difficulties or self-concept?

_____

_____

_____

Before I move on to tell you the second story, I want to share "Footprints" with you. This is an amazing little story that I first heard from a recovering addict whom I used to work with. You may know this tale, because it's on cards and bookmarks in many stores. But I'm including a short summary of it here because if you *aren't* aware of it and have some faith in God, you might find it helpful whenever you're feeling particularly overwhelmed or challenged—I know that I do.

> A man dreamed that he was walking along the beach with the Lord as he saw moments from his past. There were often two sets of footprints in the sand: his and the Lord's. But sometimes there was only one set of marks, often during the most trying experiences.
>
> He asked about this, since the Lord had promised to be with him always. He didn't understand why he'd been left alone during his worst trials.
>
> The Lord told him that when there was only one set of footprints, it was because He was carrying the man in his arms and bringing him to safety.

I love the image of being carried in times of great need. In fact, before I'd ever even heard of "Footprints," I used to envision and feel myself resting in the hands of God whenever I was overwhelmed. I think the image came to me from hearing the song "He's Got the Whole World in His Hands," where, you may remember, there's also a line about the "tiny little baby in His hands." I see and feel these huge hands, cupped lovingly together, as I—tiny in comparison—sit or lie within them. Does an image like that comfort you? Think about it. If so, use it to soothe, heal, grow, and empower you as you work to take charge of your emotional life.

BRINGING MEANING TO LIFE: JULIETTE'S STORY

Juliette was 58 years old and married, without children, when she was referred to me by her gynecologist. She had severe pelvic pain but no identifiable problem; all her examinations and medical tests were normal, so her doctor wasn't sure what to do. He'd given her medication for her pain, but nothing seemed to help.

When Juliette came to see me, I saw a beautiful, fit, and friendly woman who was quite anxious and prone to tears. "I'm not sure what to do," she told me. "I'm in constant pain, and nothing seems to help much. When I take enough medicine to control it, I can't stay awake. This is just awful."

Juliette began to tell me her story. She'd been raised with minimal exposure to her religion and didn't believe in God. She liked the holidays but didn't know much about their origins or purpose. She'd retired from a satisfying and successful career in the financial industry when the bank she worked for had been acquired two years before. She took an early retirement plan that was too good to pass up, but she was now feeling sort of lost.

She was also disturbed about her path and legacy. "I'm not sure what I'm meant to be doing with my life," she said. "I don't feel that I've made—or will make—much difference in the world. I never had kids because my husband didn't want them, so there's nothing there either. And I'm anxious all the time."

I began to wonder if Juliette's pain and excessive worry were due to a lack of meaning in her life. She met diagnostic criteria for panic disorder, but the anxiety attacks had begun around the time of her retirement. She'd never had such symptoms before. And interestingly enough, her pelvic pain had appeared soon thereafter.

I began to explore this idea with her. At first, she doubted the possibility, but as time went on, it began to make sense to her. I gave her anti-anxiety medication to use as needed and taught her how to employ thought stopping and affirmations to decrease her worry. With these tools, she improved a great deal, but her problems didn't resolve completely until she began bringing meaning and spirit-nurturing activities into her life.

So what did she do? She explored a lot of things, adding one pursuit after another, staying with those that felt satisfying or nurturing and abandoning the ones that didn't. Ultimately, Juliette chose to sponsor a child in need in another country, volunteer regularly at a local soup kitchen, plant a garden, and practice tai chi. After doing those four things for about six months, her anxiety and pelvic pain disappeared. She still participates in these activities, and to this day—several years since her graduation from my care—she's pain and panic free.

Do you relate to Juliette's story? Might you do well to bring more meaningful pursuits and spiritual practices into your Take-Charge plan? Write your reflections below or on a separate piece of paper.

_____

_____

_____

Before we go on, I need to say something to those of you who've had negative experiences with religion. If there's something particularly traumatic or tough to get past in your history, don't despair. Start with what's comfortable for you now. Do nothing that feels wrong, and be open to seeking counseling if you get to a point where that calls to you. You can use a therapist, counselor, or spiritual director—whatever feels right. It's also possible to work this step without a God-focus at all. Just look at the list in the next section, and you'll find that very few of the suggestions are religion or God oriented. You can find your way!

SUGGESTION LIST: WAYS TO CULTIVATE A SPIRITUAL CONNECTION

While I can't tell you exactly what to do to bring meaning, hope, and purpose into your Take-Charge program, I can offer you the following list of 24 things you can do to enhance your spiritual life. These are all simply suggestions, so pick out the ones that speak to you and try using them. See what works for you in building your Step 10 plan. Be open and notice what happens.

1. Give thanks. Take time to notice what works in your life. What do you appreciate? Commit to saying "Thank you" to someone every day, or send a message saying "Thank you for being in my life" to a friend, relative, or co-worker. Start a gratitude list and write down three things you're thankful for each day.

2. Help others. Decide to practice small acts of kindness, such as opening the door for someone pushing a stroller or carrying a bag of groceries. Cook dinner for a friend who's ill, volunteer your time at Habitat for Humanity, or donate money to a worthy cause. Make giving a daily practice.

3. Forgive yourself/others. Ironically, in forgiving others, we receive the benefits of health and inner peace. Sometimes we can't bless those who have hurt us until we've honored our hurt, pain, and anger and found appropriate ways to work through it. But we *can* shift our focus to compassion and forgiveness. Ask yourself, *Do I have room in my heart to forgive?* Strive to make that space. As you do, avoid fanning the flames of hurt and anger. Be gentle with yourself and others; cultivate compassion.

4. Love. You've already devoted a full step to building connection, but you may not have recognized the spiritual nature of loving and being cared for in return. All spiritual traditions revolve around the power of this emotion. Tell someone dear to you "I love you," or reach out and show how you feel.

5. Nurture acceptance. So often we strive to control or change what isn't in our power to effect. Remind yourself that you are *as you're meant to be.* Let those parts of yourself that you don't like—but can't alter—be okay. See if you can begin to tolerate them, then accept them, and ultimately, grow to love them (and yourself) fully. Let others and the universe around you just be. Stop trying to change those who hurt you. Care for yourself by altering what you have the power to effect, and simply make some space between yourself and those who unsettle you. Accept what is without judgment.

6. Study, learn, and expand your awareness. Study the Bible, spiritual or religious books, philosophy, or theology. Open yourself to the wisdom of ancient texts, traditions, practices, and laws of life. Challenge yourself to apply some of their enduring lessons to your current experiences.

7. Cultivate humility and banish judgment. You're both a wondrous being and a tiny piece of the infinite, so don't allow yourself to become too self-important. We're all of equal value. Catch yourself when you start thinking that you know better or *are* better than someone else. Ask yourself on a regular basis *Am I humble enough? Do I sound critical or judgmental?* Monitor yourself daily for arrogant thinking and behavior.

8. Don't criticize. I love the lesson that Thumper's mother teaches him in the film *Bambi,* which I remember as "If you don't have anything nice to say, don't say anything at all." We're so quick to criticize, attack, and find fault with others. Practice raising your concerns with those who hurt or anger you in a respectful way. Use this template: "When you_____, I feel _____," to confront them. Always ask yourself, *Am I being respectful in my communication?* If the answer is no, apologize and try again!

9. Look for the blessing in challenging, painful, or difficult situations. As my dad lay dying of cancer recently, my heart was breaking. He was "my person," my champion, support, and soul mate in a very profound way. He and I were the only two in my immediate family of origin who believed in God, felt comfort in our faith tradition, and shared a commitment to helping those less fortunate.

In one way, living through my father's decline was one of the most challenging and deeply painful experiences I've ever endured, but it was probably one of the most healing as well. During that time, we had so many conversations about our history, relationship, mistakes, regrets, and love. Everything that had ever hurt me in my 47-year history with him was healed in those final months. And as we sat together, my dad often said, "I so enjoy these conversations we're having," and so did I.

The fact that my father was meant to leave this earthly life because of what felt to me like an early call "Home" was deeply challenging for me. But I searched for, and found, amazing blessings in my loss. And as you know from this book's dedication, my dad did, too.

He died "ecstatic" that I was helping so many people, feeling deeply loved, and without fear. *"Adonai li v'lo y'rah,"* he would say. "My Lord is with me; I will not be afraid."

You can find blessings in the smallest of life's challenges and in the greatest experiences of pain. Look for the silver lining of every cloud, the rainbow after each storm, and the present in every loss. There's always a blessing there.

10. Search for the divine and the wonder in others. There's an ancient Jewish parable about a community where no one was getting along; there was abuse, violence, and stealing. The inhabitants began to call out, crying to God for the Messiah to come—to transform the community and bring peace. A message came back: *The Messiah is among you.*

Not knowing who it was, each villager began to treat all the others with the love and respect due to a messenger of God. Very soon, the community was transformed. Joy, respect, and compassion reigned once more, and there was no longer a need to be rescued. This change in perspective and behavior had healed the whole town.

This parable is no different in its message from what we learn in studies showing that teachers who think their students are smart wind up with gifted scholars, while those who think their classes are quite limited find their students failing simple exams.

We each have unique gifts. We're uplifted and transformed when we look at ourselves and others that way. Search for the wonder in yourself and in those you meet, reminding yourself to do this on a regular basis. You'll be amazed at what comes back if you do.

11. Always give the benefit of the doubt. Assume the best of others until proven otherwise. We're so quick to assume the worst of others. We can't find a ring, and before searching our drawers, we assume that our housekeeper took it. We don't receive an invitation to a close friend's party, and without checking out what happened, we decide that she's trying to get back at us for something. We're passed over for a promotion—for a job we're actually ill suited to perform—but decide that our boss is trying to get us to quit. . . . I could go on and on, but you get the idea.

Start to notice how often you assume the worst, and commit to challenging yourself whenever you see it happening. Ask yourself, *Do I know that for sure? What if I were to give the benefit of the doubt?* Change your behavior and change your life.

12. Pray: Offer thanks and ask for strength, wisdom, acceptance, and healing of self/others. Prayer changes lives. You may know that already, and perhaps you even pray sometimes. I suggest that if this resonates for you, plan to pray daily. Take a moment or two each morning or evening to offer thanks or ask for strength. Talk to God or your personal Higher Power. This communion with something larger than yourself will heal you.

13. Exercise, dance, meditate, or do yoga or tai chi. Many people find that settling into their bodies in these ways connects them with what's healing in the universe. Find an activity that does that for you and use it regularly. Make it part of your plan, routine, and schedule, growing into it and through it. You'll love the results!

14. Spend time being present in nature. Sometimes when I feel down or distressed, I push myself to get out. Even if I spend just a few minutes walking among the birds and cacti around my home, I feel renewed. There's something about Mother Nature's work that calms and heals us. Gazing up at the tiny arc of the moon in the night sky, walking through a carpet of wildflowers at dusk, or sitting on a mountaintop at sunrise and feeling the breeze can be awe inspiring and deeply grounding at the same time.

Commit to spending some time in the natural playground each week, and pay attention to the wonder of the scene and space. Notice the scent of a flower, the shape of a cloud, the pattern of leaves on a tree, or the sound of water rushing over smooth rocks in a stream. Be in nature—really *be* there, and be uplifted!

15. Be generous with your time, resources, and spirit. We're so quick to focus on why we can't share and spend almost no energy trying to figure out how we can do more. But our strategy is a recipe for disaster. The tighter we hold on to what we have—the more we close our hands into fists—the less we ultimately end up with. We destroy what *is* there. Yet the more we open ourselves to those around us, the more we get back. We increase our material and spiritual resources by sharing them.

You probably know the expression "If you need something done, ask a busy person." That seems counterintuitive. Shouldn't these folks have less time? Not according to the spiritual laws of the universe. You see, the more we do, the more we're able to do; the more we give, the more we get.

Devote some thought to how often you say "I can't" when asked to share your time, resources, or spirit. Figure out how you can say yes more often, and then open your hands and heart more regularly.

16. Visualize yourself in the palm of God's hand. This is the lesson of "Footprints," the story you read a summary of earlier in this chapter. If being carried, buoyed, or supported physically by God or some other loving being comforts you, then visualize yourself there. Allow yourself to see and feel the experience. Call it up whenever you feel the need for protection, love, or support; it's always available to you.

17. Paint, draw, sing, sculpt, garden, or write. These are, of course, all art forms. And for many people, something deeply spiritual happens when they enter the creative process. A bigger force takes over and expresses itself as the separation between artist and art disappears. The creator is elevated by this experience. If any form of art appeals to you, start puttering around with it. Perhaps you'll find something to do on a regular basis that heals, uplifts, and empowers you. If you do, use it!

18. Listen and receive another in pain. Really hear the story. You already know from your Step 8 work how important it is to share stories and build connections, but there's something particularly healing in receiving someone else in pain. We're touched at a deep, heart-healing level when we're really there for another in that way.

We often withdraw from people when we believe they're in pain. We tell ourselves, *I don't want to make them feel worse by coming around or asking them how they're doing.* But when we run for cover at these times, we're copping out and abandoning those who need us. Challenge yourself to call or stop by when you hear of a friend's loss or other challenge. Don't assume that someone's cancer diagnosis, death in the family, or loss of a job means that she needs space. Call her and make room for sharing. Let her tell you what she needs to say. You'll be healed for being there.

19. Explore spiritual homes, religious institutions, or Quaker meetings. Begin a regular ritual practice. You can't find your spiritual home if you don't go searching for it, and you won't feel connected to that community if you don't regularly engage in any of its ritual practices. So start visiting different churches, synagogues, ashrams, prayer groups, bible-study classes, Quaker meetings, or any other institutions that could be options for you. Talk to congregants, other participants, leaders, and clergy to find a good fit. Then begin a regular practice.

20. Feed yourself well—treat your body with the respect of good nutrition. Your physical self is the temple that houses your soul or spirit, and nurturing yourself spiritually means treating your body with respect and care.

Do you eat healthfully, getting enough fruits, vegetables, good protein sources, fats, and carbohydrates? Do you eat a lot of junk food? Take a careful inventory of your diet, and resolve to improve your nutrition a little bit at a time.

21. Surround yourself with people who believe in you. You can't cultivate faith if you're immersed in criticism, doubt, and negativity, so examine the company you keep. Work actively and aggressively to cultivate nurturing relationships, and avoid those that hold you back.

22. Nurture hope. This is one of the most crucial suggestions I have to offer you. As you know, belief in what could be heals people, and a lack of it kills them. Do everything you can to be hopeful. Read inspirational literature, listen to speakers who encourage you to trust in possibility and potential, surround yourself with optimistic friends, and only go to doctors who believe in your healing powers.

Avoid doom-and-gloom news, people, movies and Websites. Stick your head in the sand if you have to at times! Negativity is rampant in our culture, and sometimes we have to play ostrich to get away from it all.

Remember, you're wonderful. You *can* take charge of your emotional life and be well. Where there's a will, there's a way. Don't allow yourself to believe those folks who tell you otherwise.

23. Ask for help. You'll be answered. The universe wants you to be well. Don't let yourself get stuck in thinking: *No one cares, I deserve to suffer,* or *I ought to be past this need by now.* Push yourself to find the support that's waiting for you. Reach out; try, try, and try again. With persistence, you *will* be answered.

24. Never give up. I believe in you and know that you can heal. You can take charge of your emotional life. You have the ability to overcome your anxiety, distress, and depression through whole-person healing. There's always help, and there's always hope for you. If you don't believe me, read my first book; immerse yourself in its powerful tales of transformation. If those folks can do it, so can you! Have no doubt: *You can transform your life.*

I've given you 24 suggestions for ways to cultivate your spiritual connection. I could go on, but it's time for me to stop. Your inner wisdom is aching to point you in the right direction. Now you can begin to create your own spirit-care plan. Think about what you've learned in this chapter. What do you need to do to nurture your spirit? What are you ready and willing to take on? What might you choose to do in the future? Record your thoughts below or on a separate piece of paper.

_____

_____

_____

Congratulations! You've just finished a comprehensive ten-step plan to take charge of your emotional life. You'll need to revisit and work with these steps forever, but you've come a long way in healing yourself already. I'm proud of your accomplishments.

In the Afterword that follows this chapter, you'll have a chance to review what you've learned in the Take-Charge program. After revisiting each step, you'll create your own Take-Charge mission statement—your personal summary and action plan. But, before we move on, I'd like to close this step with my blessing to you.

My Prayer for You

May you live to see your dreams fulfilled.
May you appreciate your wonder, your bountiful gifts.
May you recognize your divinity reflected back at you.
And may love, hope, and purpose suffuse your being.
Amen.

AFTERWORD

It's time for you to review each of the ten steps of your Take-Charge program. Read through each one as listed below and think about what you want to do in order to work that step. You might find it helpful to revisit the appropriate chapters to refresh your memory. Record your observations and plans for each step in the space provided or on a separate piece of paper.

Step 1: Consider your story and its lessons: Do you have a medical condition or chemical imbalance?

_____

_____

_____

Step 2: Explore your need for medication.

_____

_____

_____

Step 3: Follow treatment guidelines when medication is necessary.

_____

_____

_____

Step 4: Include complementary and alternative interventions.

_____

_____

_____

Step 5: Make life choices that fit your nature.

_____

_____

_____

Step 6: Identify the beliefs that imprison you and reprogram the brain circuits involved.

_____

_____

_____

Step 7: Learn the language of your body and make friends with your inner healer.

_____

_____

_____

Step 8: Share stories and build connection.

_____

_____

_____

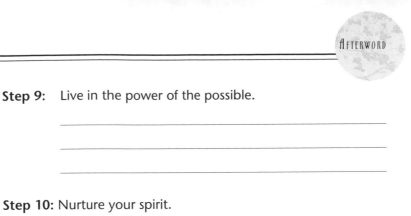

Step 9: Live in the power of the possible.

_____

_____

_____

Step 10: Nurture your spirit.

_____

_____

_____

Now review your reflections and write your personal Take-Charge mission statement below or on a separate piece of paper.

My Take-Charge Plan

In reviewing my history, I realize that I need and want to do the following:

_____

_____

_____

_____

_____

_____

_____

_____

I understand that my needs and my plan will change over time. I commit to working on what I've written now, and to altering my plan as it makes sense to do so in the future.

I can take charge of my emotional life. I can overcome anxiety, distress, and depression. I will heal.

Now, make some copies of your Take-Charge plan. Post a few in prominent places, and carry one with you wherever you go. Read and work your plan daily, updating and changing it as you grow. In this way, you'll take charge. You'll overcome your challenges, find fulfillment, and heal! You're amazing and deserve to be well. My hopes and prayers are with you.

— **Eve A. Wood, M.D.**

GLOSSARY

Acupuncture ("AK-yoo-pungk-cher") is a method of healing developed in China at least 2,000 years ago. Today, this word describes a family of procedures involving stimulation of anatomical points on the body using a variety of techniques. American practices incorporate medical traditions from China, Japan, Korea, and other countries. The technique that has been most studied scientifically involves penetrating the skin with thin, solid, metallic needles that are manipulated by the hands or electrical stimulation.

Aromatherapy ("ah-roam-uh-THER-ah-py") involves the use of essential oils (extracts or essences) from flowers, herbs, and trees to promote health and well-being.

Ayurveda ("ah-yur-VAY-dah") is an alternative medical system that has been practiced primarily on the Indian subcontinent for 5,000 years. It includes diet and herbal remedies and emphasizes the use of body, mind, and spirit in disease prevention and treatment.

Chiropractic ("kie-roh-PRAC-tic") is an alternative medical system. It focuses on the relationship between bodily structure (primarily that of the spine) and function and how that relationship affects the preservation and restoration of health. Chiropractors use manipulative therapy as an integral treatment tool.

Dietary supplements were defined by congress in the Dietary Supplement Health and Education Act (DSHEA) of 1994. A dietary supplement is a product (other than tobacco) taken by mouth that contains a "dietary ingredient" intended to supplement what you eat. Ingredients may include vitamins; minerals; herbs or other botanicals; amino acids; and substances such as enzymes, organ tissues, and metabolites. These supplements come in many forms, including extracts, concentrates, tablets, capsules, gelcaps, liquids, and powders; they have special requirements for labeling. Under DSHEA, dietary supplements are considered foods, not drugs.

Electromagnetic fields (EMFs, also called "electric and magnetic fields") are invisible lines of force that surround all electrical devices; the Earth also produces them. Electric fields are created when there's thunderstorm activity, and magnetic fields are believed to be produced by electric currents flowing at the Earth's core.

Homeopathic ("home-ee-oh-PATH-ic") **medicine** is an alternative medical system. In this discipline, there's a belief that "like cures like," meaning that small, highly diluted quantities of medicinal substances are given to cure symptoms, when the same substances given at higher or more-concentrated doses would actually cause those same symptoms.

Massage ("muh-SAHJ") therapists manipulate muscle and connective tissue to enhance function of those tissues and promote relaxation and well-being.

Naturopathic ("nay-chur-o-PATH-ic") **medicine,** or naturopathy, is an alternative medical system proposing that there's a healing power in the body that establishes, maintains, and restores health. Practitioners work with the patient with a goal of supporting this energy through treatments such as nutrition-and-lifestyle counseling, dietary supplements, medicinal plants, exercise, homeopathy, and traditional Chinese medicine.

Osteopathic ("ahs-tee-oh-PATH-ic") **medicine** is a form of conventional medicine that, in part, emphasizes diseases arising in the musculoskeletal system. There's an underlying belief that all of the body's systems work together, and disturbances in one system may affect function elsewhere. Some practitioners use osteopathic manipulation, a full-body system of hands-on techniques to alleviate pain, restore function, and promote health and well-being.

Qi gong ("chee-GUNG") is a component of traditional Chinese medicine that combines movement, meditation, and regulation of breathing to enhance the flow of *qi* (an ancient term given to what's believed to be vital energy) in the body, improve blood circulation, and enhance immune function.

Reiki ("RAY-kee") is a Japanese word representing Universal Life Energy. The practice is based on the belief that when spiritual energy is channeled through a practitioner, the patient's spirit is healed, which in turn heals the physical body.

Therapeutic touch is derived from an ancient technique called "laying-on of hands." It's based on the premise that it's the healing force of the therapist that affects the patient's recovery. Healing is promoted when the body's energies are in balance, and by passing their hands over the patient, practitioners can identify energy imbalances.

Traditional Chinese medicine (TCM) is the current name for an ancient system of health care from China. TCM is based on a concept of balanced qi (pronounced "chee"), or vital energy, that's believed to flow throughout the body. This is thought to regulate a person's spiritual, emotional, mental, and physical balance and to be influenced by the opposing forces of yin (negative energy) and yang (positive energy). Disease is thought to result from the flow of qi being disrupted and yin and yang becoming imbalanced. Among the components of TCM are herbal and nutritional therapy, restorative physical exercises, meditation, acupuncture, and remedial massage.

INDEX

A

AA (Alcoholics Anonymous), 29
Academy for Guided
    Imagery, 83
acceptance
    nurturing, 209
    sharing with others and,
    161–62
Adderall, 51
addictions, 28–29
    resources, 29
A.D.D. Warehouse, 27
adjustment disorder with
    anxious mood, 34
adversity, overcoming, 173–74
affirmations, 119–20, 127–29,
    191–92, 205
    illness and, 148
Al-Anon/Alateen, 29
alcohol, 28
allopathic medicine, 62
alternative medical systems, 64

Amen, Daniel
    Healing ADD, 75–76
    Healing Anxiety and
    Depression, 75–76
American Journal of Psychiatry,
    52
American Massage Therapy
    Association (AMTA), 84
American Music Therapy
    Association, 72
antidepressants, 38, 52–53
anxiety disorders, 11–12
    medication and, 52
Anxiety Disorders Association
    of America, 18, 21, 24
Archives of General Psychiatry,
    27
Art of Living Foundation, 74
assuming the worst, 183–84
assumptions, faulty, 106,
    115–16
Ativan, 51

attention deficit disorder (ADD), 91
    medications and, 51–53
attention-deficit/hyperactivity
    disorder (ADHD), 12, 24–25
    checklist, 26
    resources, 26–27
awareness, expanding, 210
Ayurveda, 70

B

B₁₂ and folate, 78
Beinfield, Harriet: *Between Heaven
    and Earth*, 70
being present, 166
being there for others, 168
benefit of the doubt, 211–12
Benson, Herbert, 81
Between Heaven and Earth (Beinfield,
    Korngold), 70
bioelectromagnetic-based therapies, 65
biofield therapies, 65
biologically based therapies, 65,
    76–79
    resources, 78
bipolar disorder, 14–16
body-speak, 142
    affirmations, 148–49
    identifying, 146–47
    psychotherapy and, 148–49
Brown, Richard, 74

C

CAM. *See* complementary and
    alternative medicine (CAM)
CAM on PubMed, 78

catastrophizing, 124
Centers for Disease Control, 83
checklists
    attention-deficit/hyperactivity
        disorder (ADHD), 26
    depression symptoms, 13–14
    generalized anxiety disorder
        (GAD), 23
    manic-depressive illness, 15–16
    obsessive-compulsive disorder, 19
    post-traumatic stress disorder
        (PTSD), 20–21
    social phobia, 22
Children and Adults with Attention-
    Deficit/Hyperactivity Disorder,
    27
Chopra, Deepak, 70
clarity, sharing with others and, 163
Cleveland Clinic Health Information
    Center, 86
Columbia University, 86
company you keep, monitoring,
    188–89, 214
complementary and alternative
    medicine (CAM), 63–66
    experiences and interventions,
    66
    use of, 68–69
connecting with others, 168–69,
    172
    template for, 165
    tools and strategies for, 165–72
Consider-the-Possibilities exercise,
    180–92
creativity, 213
criticizing others, 210

D

DA (Debtors Anonymous), 29
depression, 5, 11–12
    commonality of, 12–13
    kinds of, 13–14
    medications and, 51–53
    resources, 14
    symptom checklist, 13–14
Depression and Bipolar Support
    Alliance, 16
Descartes, René, 62
Dexedrine, 53
diagnoses
    inappropriate, 3–6
    psychiatrists and, 10–12
*Diagnostic and Statistical Manual of
    Mental Disorders (DSM)*, 11, 29
difficulties, blessings in, 210–11
direct effect medications, 50
divine in others, the, 211
Driven to Distraction (Hallowell,
    Ratey), 27
drugs, proper use of, 1
DSM. *See Diagnostic and Statistical
    Manual of Mental Disorders
    (DSM)*

E

energy therapies, 65, 70
essence and life choices, 98–99
Essential Spirituality (Walsh), 195–96
exercise, 80, 212
exercises, 39–41, 80
    Consider-the-Possibilities,
    180–87

Guided Imagery for Honoring
    Your Body's Language, 151–52
My Body Talks, 143–45
Rediscovering Me, 95–98
Sentence-Completion, 125–26
Spiritual Assessment, 201–3
Time Travel, 143

F

failure
    fear of, 106
    and opportunity, 185–86
fear, 121
    of failure, 106
    managing, 106
feelings, sharing of, 166–67
finding your path, 93–95
"Footprints," 206, 213
forgiveness, 209
Freedom from Fear, 18

G

GA (Gamblers Anonymous), 29
gardens, planting, 170
general health assessments, 29–30
generalized anxiety disorder (GAD),
    4, 23, 37
    checklist, 23
    resources, 23–24
generosity, 213
genes, 7–8
Gerbarg, Patricia, 74
"Get the Facts" (NCCAM), 62–63
Gibran, Kahlil: *The Prophet*, 203
grief, 5

groups, joining, 169
guided imagery, 82–83
    resources, 83
Guided Imagery for Honoring Your
    Body's Language exercise,
    151–52
guidelines, consider the possibilities,
    180–92
guilt, 121–22
Gulf War syndrome, 3

H

Hallowell, Edward M.: *Driven to
    Distraction*, 27
healing, faith and, 204–6
Healing ADD (Amen), 75–76
Healing Anxiety and Depression
    (Amen), 75–76
Healing Mind, The, 83
Healing Your Body, Mind, and Spirit,
    140–41
Health Journeys, 83
help, asking for, 215
helping others, 209
hidden beliefs, 117–19
Hippocrates, 61, 83
holistic medicine, 61
home environment, self-concept
    and, 112–13
hope, nurturing, 214–15
humility, 210
hyperactivity, 24

I

illness, roots of, 7–8, 147

impulsivity, 25
inattention, 24
indirect effect medications, 50–51
inner healer, 4, 136, 145, 150, 197
    language of, 133, 151
    Sandra and, 138–39
insanity, 107
internalized messages, 111–14
International Arts-Medicine
    Association, 72
International Foundation for
    Research and Education on
    Depression, 14

K

King and I, The, 72
Korngold, Efrem, 70

L

light therapy, 85–86
    resources, 86
limitations, perceiving, 106
listening, 166–67, 213–14
Little Engine That Could, The, 174–75
loneliness and isolation, 153–57
love, 209
Love and Survival (Ornish), 83, 154

M

manic-depressive illness, 14–16, 45
    checklist, 15–16
    kinds of, 16
    medication and, 53
    resources, 16

manipulative and body-based methods, 65
massage, 83–85
   resources, 84
Massage Magazine, 84
"Massage Strategies for Depressed Patients," 83
Massage Therapy Journal, 83
Mayo Clinic, 86
medications
   choosing, 57
   direct effect medications, 50
   dosages, 54–55
   duration of use, 57–58
   evaluation guidelines, 53, 55–56
   family background and, 32–36
   four principles and, 36–37
   indirect effect, 50–51
   need for, 1, 34–35
   overview questions, 60
   recap, 60
   risk-benefit consideration, 44–45
   side effects and, 44, 45–46
   specific diagnosis and, 37–38
   specificity and, 42–43
   starting and stopping, 58
   target symptoms and, 39–41
   treatment guidelines, 49, 51–52
meditative relaxation response, 81
mental illnesses, 27–28
mind-body interventions, 64
Mind/Body Medical Institute, 81
Molecules of Emotion (Pert), 71–72
mood swings, 12, 14–16
motivations of others, 184–85

music, 71–73
   resources, 72
My Body Talks exercise, 143–45

N

NA (Narcotics Anonymous), 29
Naparstek, Belleruth, 82
National Alliance on Mental Illness (NAMI), 14
National Center for Complementary and Alternative Medicine (NCCAM), 62–63
   Clearinghouse, 65–66
   "Get the Facts," 62–63
National Certification Board for Therapeutic Massage and Bodywork (NCBTMB), 84
National Council on Alcoholism and Drug Dependence, 29
National Institute of Mental Health (NIMH), 14
National Institute on Alcohol Abuse and Alcoholism, 29
National Institutes of Health (NIH), 12
nature, presence in, 212
negative self-talk, transforming, 127–29
negative thoughts, 124–25, 175
negativity, sharing with others and, 161
Northrup, Christiane: *Wisdom of Menopause*, 75–76
nutrition, 76-76, 214

O ❦

OA (Overeaters Anonymous), 29
obsessive-compulsive disorder, 18
    checklist, 19
    resources, 19
Office of Dietary Supplements,
    National Institutes of Health, 78
omega-3 fatty acids, 78–79
    resources, 79
opening up to others, 168
Ornish, Dean: *Love and Survival*, 83,
    154
overgeneralization, 123–24

P ❦

pain, origins of, 4–5
panic disorder, 17
    checklist, 17–18
    resources, 18
partnerships, creating, 171–72
passions, pursuing, 91-93
past, examining, 101
patience, 108–9, 190
perfectionism, 109
perseverance, 215
perspective, sharing stories and, 160
Pert, Candace, 134
    Molecules of Emotion, 71–72
pessimistic thinking, 122–23
pets, caring for, 170–71
physical messages, 133–35
Physicians' Desk Reference (PDR), 55
post-traumatic stress disorder
    (PTSD), 3, 19–20, 141
    checklist, 20–21
    resources, 21

prayer, 212
presenting complaints, identifying,
    6–7
    ten questions, 9–10
priorities, 107–8
program goals, 9
progress, recognizing, 108–9
progressive muscle relaxation, 81–82
Prophet, The (Gibran), 203
Prozac, 54
pursuing our passions, 91–93

Q ❦

qi gong, 70

R ❦

Ratey, John J.: *Driven to Distraction*,
    27
rebound anxiety, 52
Rediscovering Me exercise, 95–98
reductionist medicine, 62
Reiki, 70
relaxation techniques and guided
    imagery, 80–83
resources. *See also under name of*
    person or organization
    addictions, 29
    attention-deficit/hyperactivity
    disorder (ADHD), 26–27
    biologically based therapies, 78
    depression, 14
    generalized anxiety disorder
    (GAD), 23–24
    guided imagery, 83
    light therapy, 86
    manic-depressive illness, 16

massage, 84

music, 72

obsessive-compulsive disorder, 19

omega-3 fatty acids, 79

panic disorder, 18

post-traumatic stress disorder (PTSD), 21

social phobia, 22

Ritalin, 51, 53

ritual practice, 214

roadblocks, 103–10

S

Saint-John's Wort, 76–77

SAM-e, 77–78

seasonal affective disorder (SAD), 85–86

self-concept, origins of, 112–13

self-devaluation, 121

self-knowledge, importance of, 90–93

Sentence-Completion exercise, 125–26

serotonin, 82

sharing

acceptance and, 161

clarity and, 162–63

dreams, 189

intimacy and, 163–65

negativity and, 160–61

perspective and, 159–60

stories, 157

side effects, 44, 45–46, 55

SLAA (Sex and Love Addiction Anonymous), 29

social phobia, 21

checklist, 22

resources, 22

Society for the Arts in Healthcare, 72

somatization, 135

Sound of Music, 1, 8

Spiritual Assessment exercise, 201–3

spirituality

central messages, 195

enhancing, 208–15

and health, 193–95

practices, benefits of, 196

principles, 196–99

religion and, 199–200

"stinking thinking," 115

Stop Anxiety Now Kit (Wood), 18, 23, 81, 138

stories

author, 32–33, 59, 86, 91-93, 135–37, 159-60, 176–79

Ben (others remind us), 158-59

Carol (powerful transformation), 129–31

Christina (an ongoing experience), 34–35, 38 39, 41

Daniel (panic attacks), 42–43

Denise (assuming the worst), 183–84

Frank (recognizing external stressors), 139–40

Fred (consider the possibilities), 180–82

Gabe (misconceptions, breaking free from), 114–15, 158

Georgette (motivations of others), 184–85

Greg (expectations of deterioration), 3–4

Jake (origins of pain), 4–5, 8, 37, 43
  John (healing lessons from the past), 145–46
  Juliette (bringing meaning to life), 207–8
  lessons of, 6–7
  Lisa (separating the past and present), 139–40
  Melissa (hidden beliefs), 117–19
  Miguel (faith heals), 204–6
  Pamela (help along the path), 33–34, 38
  Rhonda (lingering grief), 5, 8, 39–40
  Sandra (worrying herself sick), 137–39
  sharing of, 157–59
  Stan (discovering the lost self), 100–101, 116–17
Sudarshan Kriya (SKY), 74
sweating the small stuff, 182–83
symptoms
  identifying, 1
  list of, 41
  monitoring, 48
  rating scale, 42
  target symptoms, 39–42

T

template for connecting with others, 165
thankfulness, 209
There's Always Help; There's Always Hope (Wood), 2, 4, 12, 26, 90, 101, 138, 160
thoughts, imprisoning, 120

Time Travel exercise, 143
Touch Research Institutes (TRI), 84
Transcendental Meditation (TM), 81

U

"Use of Complementary and Alternative Medicine in the United States" survey, 67–69

V

Valium, 51
visualizing success, 190–91
visualization for healing, 126–27

W

Walsh, Roger: *Essential Spirituality*, 195–96
Websites. *See name of person or organization; under* resources
Wisdom of Menopause (Northrup), 75–76
wishes, recognition of, 179–80
Wood, Eve A.
  Stop Anxiety Now Kit, 18, 23, 81, 138
  stories, 32–33, 135–37
  There's Always Help; There's Always Hope, 2, 4, 12, 26, 90, 101, 138, 160, 177
  Website, 12, 14, 16, 18, 19, 21, 22, 24, 27

Y

yoga, 73–75

ACKNOWLEDGMENTS

Whenever I write, teach, or parent, I put my whole self in. I don't know how to do it any other way. I share my perspective, but I also go out on a limb and reveal my own pain, joy, secrets, and ongoing challenges. In doing so, I make myself vulnerable to the world.

There's a part of this that's scary. As a result, I'm eternally grateful to those who support and encourage me in my work. I need every one of you to enable me to pursue my mission, which is to help as many people as possible heal or become whole in a broken world.

I must start by thanking Reid Tracy, the president of Hay House and a wonderful human being. Reid saw the power and potential of my work and welcomed me into my new home. He has been a champion and a great support. I adore him.

Hay House is an author's dream. Every single person I've had the pleasure of working with since June 2005 has enriched my life and work. You are Jacqui Clark, Georgene Cevasco, Rocky George, Amy Gingery, Roberta Grace, Louise Hay, Jill Kramer, Nancy Levin, Jeannie Liberati, Shannon Littrell, Summer McStravick, Diane Ray, Kyle Rector, Christy Salinas, Sonny Salinas, Stacey Smith, John Thompson, Angela Torrez, and Jessica Vermooten. It's not often that an author has the pleasure of developing true friendships with those behind the scenes of her work. But I feel so blessed to have my editor Jill, publicist Angela, producer Diane, and event coordinator Nancy in my life. Thank you all for your wisdom, support, and love.

I am also awed and grateful for the caring and encouragement of my colleague friends Victoria Maizes, Tieraona Low Dog, Ann Marie Chiasson, and Joan Borysenko. It's such a delight to find like-minded spirits who want you to succeed. You four are true blessings in my life.

This is the second time I've sent a brainchild out into the world for endorsements and had a series of angels step in to encourage and acknowledge my manuscript. You dear folks are Daniel Benor, Joan Borysenko, Susan Cooper, Frederic Craigie, James Lake, Tieraona Low Dog, Victoria Maizes, Michelle May, Belleruth Naparstek, Christiane Northrup, Candace Pert, and Andrew Weil. I'm grateful to every one of you for taking the time to read what I had to say and offering me such validating feedback.

While many other people support me in my efforts, there are a number of additional individuals who deserve special mention. My mother-in-law, Helene Isenberg, has been so loving and proud of me that it warms my heart. My Aunt Marcine and Uncle Arty Weiner are like second parents to me. My dear friend and publicist Cate Cummings continues to enrich my life and work. My children, Benjamin, Gabriel, Shira, and Glory, light up my life and willingly allow me to share their stories in my books. And my biggest behind-the-scenes supporter is my husband, Rick Isenberg, who keyboards every word I write and encourages me to keep going, no matter what sacrifices are involved.

I can't close the acknowledgment section of any book without thanking all of my patients. You're my greatest teachers. I offer a special thanks to those of you who have allowed me to share your stories in this book.

I must also thank my father, Leonard Wood, of blessed memory, for his past and continuing love and support; and my mother, Glory Ann Wood, God rest her soul, who believed in me from day one. I thank God for all the gifts I've been given, and thank you, my dear readers, for welcoming me into your lives.

ABOUT THE AUTHOR

Eve A. Wood, M.D., the award-winning author of *There's Always Help; There's Always Hope,* has devoted nearly two decades to the care of troubled individuals from all walks of life. Her therapeutic approach has attracted attention and acclaim from the nation's leading authorities in the fields of medicine, health, and spiritual well-being. She's the author of numerous articles for medical and professional publications, is a feature columnist for *Massage Therapy Journal,* and is a frequent speaker at national workshops and conferences. Dr. Wood is the host of a weekly call-in radio show, *Healing Your Body, Mind, and Spirit* on **HayHouse Radio.com**®.

She has served on the faculty of the University of Pennsylvania School of Medicine, the executive committee of The Institute of Pennsylvania Hospital, and is Clinical Associate Professor of Medicine at the University of Arizona Program in Integrative Medicine. Uniting body, mind, and spirit In One™ in an empowering treatment model, she helps people take charge of their emotional lives. Dr. Wood lives in Tucson with her husband and four children.

For more information, please visit: **www.DrEveWood. com**.

NOTES

We hope you enjoyed this Hay House book. If you'd like to receive a free catalog featuring additional Hay House books and products, or if you'd like information about the Hay Foundation, please contact:

Hay House, Inc.
P.O. Box 5100
Carlsbad, CA 92018-5100

(760) 431-7695 or **(800) 654-5126**
(760) 431-6948 (fax) or **(800) 650-5115 (fax)**
www.hayhouse.com® • **www.hayfoundation.org**

Published and distributed in Australia by: Hay House Australia Pty. Ltd., 18/36 Ralph St., Alexandria NSW 2015 • *Phone:* 612-9669-4299 *Fax:* 612-9669-4144 • www.hayhouse.com.au

Published and distributed in the United Kingdom by: Hay House UK, Ltd., 292B Kensal Rd., London W10 5BE • *Phone:* 44-20-8962-1230 *Fax:* 44-20-8962-1239 • www.hayhouse.co.uk

Published and distributed in the Republic of South Africa by: Hay House SA (Pty), Ltd., P.O. Box 990, Witkoppen 2068 *Phone/Fax:* 27-11-706-6612 • orders@psdprom.co.za

Published in India by: Hay House Publications (India) Pvt. Ltd., Muskaan Complex, Plot No. 3, B-2, Vasant Kunj, New Delhi 110 070 *Phone:* 91-11-4176-1620 *Fax:* 91-11-4176-1630 • www.hayhouseindia.co.in

Distributed in Canada by: Raincoast, 9050 Shaughnessy St., Vancouver, B.C. V6P 6E5 *Phone:* (604) 323-7100 • *Fax:* (604) 323-2600 • www.raincoast.com

Tune in to **HayHouseRadio.com**® for the best in inspirational talk radio featuring top Hay House authors! And, sign up via the Hay House USA Website to receive the Hay House online newsletter and stay informed about what's going on with your favorite authors. You'll receive bimonthly announcements about: Discounts and Offers, Special Events, Product Highlights, Free Excerpts, Giveaways, and more!
www.hayhouse.com®